A DEVELOPMENTAL VIEW OF THE PSYCHOANALYTIC PROCESS:

Follow-up Studies and their Consequences

A DEVELOPMENTAL VIEW OF THE PSYCHOANALYTIC PROCESS:

Follow-up Studies and Their Consequences

by

NATHAN SCHLESSINGER, M.D.
FRED P. ROBBINS, M.D.

INTERNATIONAL UNIVERSITIES PRESS, INC.

New York, New York

Copyright © 1983, Nathan Schlessinger and Fred P. Robbins.

All rights reserved. No part of this book may be reproduced by any means, nor translated into a machine language, without the written permission of the publisher.

Library of Congress Catalog in publication data

Schlessinger, Nathan.
    A developmental view of the psychoanalytic process.

    (Emotions and behavior; monograph 1)
Includes bibliograhical references and index.
    1. Psychoanalysis—Longitudinal studies. I. Robbins,
Fred P. II. Title. III. Series. [DNLM: 1. Follow-up
studies. 2. Psychoanalysis. W1 EM672 monograph 1 /
WM 460 S342d]
RC506.S297 1983   616.89′17   83-225
ISBN 0-8236-1257-0
ISSN 0734-9890

Manufactured in the United States of America

CONTENTS

FOREWORD

The Chicago Institute for Psychoanalysis came into being in October 1932. Now, fifty years later, the pioneering spirit of clinical inquiry that characterized this educational and research institution continues in full force. Our Institute has supported and encouraged investigations by individuals and groups of all aspects of psychoanalysis. The studies of the past five decades have constituted a significant contribution to the broad base of psychoanalytic knowledge and have been usually enlightening, often provocative, and sometimes germinal in their import.

With this volume, the Institute inaugurates a series of monographs dealing with different aspects of psychoanalysis. We are very pleased that this first monograph so ideally fits our criteria for the series. It is a report of a careful psychoanalytic research project, its primary data derive from the clinic of the Chicago Institute for Psychoanalysis, the theoretical assumptions and premises are consonant with current psychoanalytic knowledge, and the authors, as well as the analysts who provided the clinical material for this study, come from our own Institute. It is indeed an auspicious way to begin our next fifty years.

Drs. Schlessinger and Robbins are engaged in an ongoing follow-up research project. Utilizing a previously introduced method of inquiry, they have developed a design, collected data, developed criteria for assessment, obtained results, and arrived at conclusions that should stimulate much discussion. Follow-up and outcome research is a means of testing our clinical and technical hypotheses. More and more we will be called upon to document our therapeutic results. This research report will undoubtedly promote further outcome and follow-up research and present a basis for arriving at current assessments of the validity of our clinical efforts.

It is a personal pleasure to introduce this first monograph of the Chicago Institute for Psychoanalysis series of *Emotions and Behavior*. It exemplifies our credo of creativity, continuity, and change in a constructive direction.

George H. Pollock, M.D., Ph.D.
Director, Institute for Psychoanalysis

July 3, 1982

Perspective

It is our purpose in this book to contribute to the evolution of a new view of psychoanalysis by exploring and documenting a particular approach to the study of the analytic process based on follow-up research and clinical investigation. We hope by this to return to the wellsprings of psychoanalysis, to observation and interpretation as they influence and interact with theory formation.

In its origins, psychoanalysis was conceived by Freud with the grand design of formulating a general psychology of human behavior. His early grasp and reach were in creative conjunction. Dreams, forgetfulness and memory, parapraxes and the enigmas of neurotic symptomtology were scrutinized in an exhilarating effort to find meaning in what was regarded as obscure, unmentionable, or unworthy of attention. Observations and interpretations were generalized and wedded to a bold and imaginative attempt, through the use of metaphor, to create a theoretical scaffolding for psychoanalysis and a series of models of the mind. Technical advances were developed and recorded in their appropriate context in the pages of his case histories. In his *Introductory Lectures*

1

(1916-1917) Freud's account of his experiences reads like a detective story as he confronts the riddles of life. The interplay of clinical experience and theoretical formulation created the rudiments of a science.

Freud's clinical theories and metapsychology generated a rich and varied yield of insights into human behavior. The past half century has seen the elaboration and development of these ideas in ego psychology, in penetrating analyses of character, in studies of transference and countertransference, in longitudinal studies based on the direct observation of children, and in self-psychology. Particularly in the clinical frame of reference there is much that is vital and productive in the widening scope of psychoanalysis. But, as Leites (1971) has pointed out in his devastating, if well-intentioned, critique of the language of analysis, the metapsychology that Freud created as a motor for the analytic enterprise became a fetter. In subtle ways it constricted the view of the analytic process. Ironically, the discoveries of yesterday were capable of transformation into ritualistic formulae that threatened to congeal the analytic process and to isolate and subdue the fresh insights issuing forth from the study of self-psychology and the various lines of development.

Freud referred to metapsychology as an analytic myth and even personified it as the "witch" of psychoanalysis. In his methodological asides, he repeatedly made clear that his conjectures and metaphors were in no way sacrosanct. For Freud, the "witch" was a creative product of his clinical experience and his imagination, and her form was subject to radical change in the further elaborations of his creativity. He could be playful with his product. It was his witch! But as we know from the tales of our childhood and our clinical experience, witches do not always serve their creators well.

Recent contributions by Basch (1976), Holt (1975),

Peterfreund (1975), and Schafer (1976) have critically examined psychoanalytic theory, giving expression to a growing discontent with metapsychology and emphasizing the unfortunate gap between it and clinical observation and interpretation. Basch notes the disparities between accumulating knowledge in neurophysiology and Freud's conceptualization of the mental apparatus. He would dispense with pseudo-neurophysiological models of the mind and regard psychoanalysis as a science of meaning, with its appropriate area of study the vicissitudes of information. Peterfreund mounts a similar attack on the bastions of metapsychology and approaches the task of reformulating psychoanalytic theory in terms of information science, in particular, an information-processing and systems model consistent with neurophysiology. Holt suggests that psychoanalysis will gradually set aside its metapsychology and treasure its clinical truth with or without a new general theory. Schafer proposes an action language to express the essence of the psychoanalytic approach in as precise and realistic a manner as possible, divested of crude metaphors that have outlived their usefulness. In this analytic dialogue, Arlow (1975) defends the structural theory, suggesting that the problem lies in Freud's having carried over into his theory of the twenties some of the metapsychological assumptions of earlier theorizing. In his view, a more precise conceptualization, stripped of biological and metapsychological speculations, would permit the structural theory to serve well as a theoretical frame of reference for psychoanalysis. Difficult problems like the stultification in the development of psychoanalysis to which we refer, invite a variety of attempts at solution, as various as those noted above—i.e., a radical change in theory, a discarding of theory altogether with attention to clinical experience, a new language to reflect the clinical experience.

The solution we would advocate—based on a developmental view of the psychoanalytic process—has its own metaphor in the current psychoanalytic approach to individual development. But, more significantly, its central direction and method is entirely consistent with the method that Freud used—that is to say, the scientific method. Let's be precise about what we mean by first describing the ways in which psychoanalysis falls short of the scientific method. In his reply to the criticism of analysis by the philosophers of science, Waelder complained that critics choose metapsychology as the ground for debate rather than lower levels of the hierarchy of theory formation, where most of the daily work of analysis resides. But Waelder's view begs the question. Much of the literature of psychoanalysis is clothed in the garb of metapsychology and even case reports are transformed and condensed into abstract language that may distort the experience it attempts to describe. Furthermore, the effort to separate metapsychology from clinical experience and clinical theory has its own pitfalls and may produce a solution that is more apparent than real. Observations and inferences are influenced in gross and subtle fashion by the frame of mind of the analyst, who is prepared to see what his theory has taught him to look for and to interpret what he has been taught to interpret. Preconceived theory is an inevitable influence on the technique and practice of psychoanalysis and the circular nature of the process must be acknowledged.

What then provides for proper sustenance and growth in psychoanalytic conceptualization? Not primarily the rigorous application of logic and the demand for internal consistency, but the courage to be surprised, to be prepared to examine clinical experience wherever it may lead and to discard or modify theories that are not borne out by facts or by scientific advances in related disciplines. Psychoanalytic education and research must be directed toward the discovery of truth, not the repetition of dogma. While the best psychoanalytic education may prove largely to be a matter of the student's rediscovering, as it were, already established basic concepts, if it is directed toward discovery in the first place rather than repetition or rote learning, the prospect of new learning is assured. It may perhaps seem a declaration of the obvious to stress such a "simple" remedy, but our reading of analytic history contradicts such a judgment and our experience suggests that there are means to apply such a remedy.

Idealization of Freud's contributions to analysis constitutes a useful element of our scientific ego ideal as long as we avoid the ritualization of content and the degradation of idealization into idolatry. In our view, the most admirable feature of Freud's creativity was his scientific style in the process of discovery itself. It is no accident that in his most creative period at the turn of the century, Freud's work was most closely allied to case reports, including the intensive study of his own dreams and experiences. In later papers, the balance shifted toward fragmentary, anecdotal accounts and clinical generalizations as the basis for theory construction. In each period of theoretical revision, however, the stimulus remained a set of contradictory observations that shook his formulations. His scientific skepticism was on the alert for contradiction as the whetstone for keen comprehension. His recognition, for example, that the reports of his patients about their early traumatic memories were not necessarily real events led to the discovery of the significance of fantasy in psychic reality and to the elaboration of an intrapsychic frame of reference for psychoanalysis.

The shift from the topographic model to the structural model was similarly motivated by clinical observations that contradicted his expectations. Forces opposed to the instincts such as the mechanisms of defense and the sense of guilt were clearly unconscious phenomena, thereby challenging the prevailing paradigm of conflict between unconscious instinctual forces and conscious or preconscious controlling forces. Other examples might readily be cited but one final one will suffice, Freud's paper "Analysis Terminable and Interminable" (1937). Freud was 81 at the time he authored this paper on the eve of the Nazi putsch. A symposium had been held recently on the theory of therapeutic effects. In a searching view of a lifetime of effort and the assessment of results, Freud chose to consider the obstacles facing psychoanalysis, its limits, and the reasons for its failure. To confront such issues under such circumstances was an affirmation of scientific ideals characteristic of Freud's indomitable spirit.

If Freud's approach were typical of the analytic enterprise today, the problems faced by psychoanalysis might be considerably lessened. For it is in the area of the critical review of outcome and process—precisely the area that Freud addressed in 1937—that the critics of analysis have their most vulnerable target. But that is a negative and defensive statement of the issue. For it is in this area, too, that analysts, by falling so far short of the scientific approach, have deprived themselves of the data and the contradictions so vital to the growth of psychoanalysis as a science. There are so many questions to be answered. What are the consequences of an analysis? How does the intrapsychic milieu change? How shall we measure change? What prompts analysands to return to their analysts? How are second analyses the same as or different from first analyses? What can we learn from our observations and inferences to enrich our store of data and challenge our ritualized explanations? How can we confront and resolve the theoretical conflicts of divergent schools in studying their effects on the analytic process?

In his role as an analytic philosopher, Waelder (1956) advised those who were interested in discovery, as a first step, to choose what was despised, shunned, disregarded, derided, and rejected, on whatever grounds, as the object of careful inquiry. With regard to outcome studies, analysts have honored this prescription largely in the breach. Lack of agreement about criteria and the multiplicity of variables to be considered have been advanced as important reasons for the woefully inadequate effort to confront problems in outcome and follow-up of psychoanalysis. Such factors might account, for a time, for problems in organizing large statistical studies. They would not explain the persistent lack in this area nor the relative dearth of individual clinical reports on experiences with results of analysis and re-analysis. A significant ingredient in the situation is the defensive posture of the analyst who knows what the outcome of analysis "ought to be" and holds himself painfully and secretly accountable for any process that falls short of goals hallowed by tradition. What a potential for growth and insight may be lost in such a quagmire!

The purpose of this book is to present our experience over the past decade with follow-up studies of analytic patients at the Clinic of The Institute for Psychoanalysis in Chicago and the effect of that experience on our view and practice of psychoanalysis as a developmental process. The studies have been intensive and analytic with a focus on the assessment of intrapsychic change in the course of an analysis and its aftermath.

We shall present a series of cases to illustrate our

findings, and then state our hypotheses and conclusions at the level of clinical theory. Conflicting paradigms have been enunciated in analytic practice in efforts to integrate the patient's early developmental vicissitudes with his structural conflicts. These vary from a sharp division into separate diagnostic categories, as in Kohut's differentiation of "tragic man" and "guilty man," through the characterization of all development as recapitulating either the resolution of the Oedipus complex along classical Freudian lines or the resolution of the earliest infantile experiences along Kleinian lines, to conceptualizations based on an integrated developmental point of view utilizing both Mahler's research on separation-individuation and Anna Freud's lines of development. Our clinical investigations have influenced us to move in the last of these directions, suggesting just such an integrated developmental view of derivative aspects of childhood experience in the analytic process. We shall elaborate such a clinical theoretical view in relation to our case material and a review of the literature on follow-up studies.

We began with an interest in the outcome of the process two to five years after the completion of an analysis. Our initial experiences confirmed Pfeffer's observations (1959) that a former patient would recapitulate his analysis in miniature in the space of a few interviews. A standard method and a set of criteria for assessing the data evolved out of the need to organize the information readily made available. Essentially, we attempted to bring the clinical approach and analytic mode of investigation to a microscopic view of significant samples of information. We established to our satisfaction that the method permitted us meaningful access to the nature of the analytic process. We could assess changes in the course of the analysis, observe the effects of the process, and gain some insight into the dynamisms involved.

The follow-up studies provided an unusual opportunity in a clinical situation to check impressions gained from a preliminary assessment of the analytic process. They served as a kind of experimental repetition in condensed form of the complex events and interactions of analysis, offering an opportunity for confirmation or refutation of established notions about the process, its curative factors, and its outcome. What is so commonly limited to the realm of introspection can be verified and tested by reexamining the patient's inner conflicts and modes of interaction as they are expressed in the research encounter.

Our findings in the successful analytic cases we studied paralleled the results of investigations by Pfeffer (1959, 1961b, 1963) and Norman, Blacker, Oremland, and Barrett (1976). Psychic conflicts were not eliminated in the analytic process. The clinical material of the follow-ups demonstrated a repetitive pattern of conflicts. Accretions of insight were evident but the more significant outcome of the analysis appeared to be the development of a preconsciously active self-analytic function, in identification with the analyzing function of the analyst, as a learned mode of coping with conflicts. As elements of the transference neurosis reappeared and were re-solved, the components of a self-analytic function were demonstrated in self-observation, reality processing, and the tolerance and mastery of frustration, anxiety, and depression. The resources gained in the analytic process persisted, and their vitality was evident in response to renewed stress.

Excited by some recurring phenomena in the follow-up studies, our attention then shifted to the fate of the analytic alliance. It is this aspect of our investigation that has been the most challenging and rewarding, providing a view of the process with significant theoretical and technical consequences. Former patients reported that in confronting problems they would utilize a "benign presence" externally or in fantasy to facilitate efforts at solution of conflict. A particular friend, a spouse, or the remembered presence of the analyst served as a useful catalyst. These descriptions underlined the significance of the analytic alliance as a matrix for the analytic process, and for the acquisition and consolidation of a self-analytic function.

As we pursued our explorations we were struck by a common problem in a number of the cases studied, cases which had been formulated in terms of an oedipal paradigm with inadequate attention to earlier developmental derivatives. The clinical issues involved were states of overstimulation, frantic efforts to ameliorate these states, and attitudes of compliance which limited the effectiveness of interpretive efforts directed at structural conflicts. In our view, the patients in these cases indicated defects in structure coexistent with psychoneurotic symptomatology and based on problems in object relations, narcissism, and separation-individuation experiences. Our studies have emphasized the need to attend to such psychopathology not simply as a regressive defense against oedipal conflict but as a significant focus of analytic interest in its own right and a critical determinant of the outcome of the process.

The analytic setting and the initiation of the process facilitate at the deepest level the engagement of the basic transference potential of the analysand toward the analyst. The regularity and frequency of sessions and the quality of the analyst's sensitive attention and tactful interventions may produce a psychotherapeutic effect that obscures pathological early developmental deriva-

tives in the analytic process. Thus, when tension-regulatory functions derived from early experience become
evident around separations and breaks in empathy, they
may be regarded merely as regressive phenomena without adequate analysis of their developmental significance. Early defects and distortions in object relations
and tension regulation create intrapsychic conditions for
intense actual neurotic states and thereby promote psychoneurotic solutions. In effect, our studies have sensitized us to the early developmental precursors of
neurosogenesis that are evident in any analytic process.
Specific patterns of child-parent interaction with regard
to expectations about separation and individuation appear to be most significantly engaged in termination. The
problem of mourning as an issue in the termination phase
can, of course, be addressed only in a preparatory way,
so that where earlier developmental derivatives have not
been acknowledged, they may become more dramatically
evident in post-analytic experiences. We have come to
conceptualize the outcome of separation-individuation
experience as the development of a self-soothing function,
and the patient's particular pattern of solving dyadic
problems as a significant forerunner of the defense transference. Analysis of the mode of tension regulation is a
necessary antecedent, we believe, to the development and
consolidation of a secure self-analytic function in confronting intrapsychic conflict.

We readily acknowledge that the view we have outlined above concerning the relationship between early
developmental defects and distortions and later neurotic
features is by no means self-evident. There are serious
theoretical issues to be considered. If there are significant
persistent dyadic problems, would oedipal conflicts develop at all? Doesn't the experience of the oedipus complex presume adequate separation-individuation? Can

one reasonably address issues of object and self constancy in an adult neurotic? Can there be regression from oedipal conflict to early developmental derivatives of the separation-individuation process? Would the derivatives of earlier conflicts remain at all discrete or be so transformed by the resolution of the oedipus complex that any effort to focus them in the analytic process would be illusory? The clinical experiences which we shall describe in this monograph suggest that pathology derived from early development may emerge in the analysis of neurotic patients with significant oedipal conflicts and may be engaged productively in the analytic process. In our view, the problems a patient presents are not *either* oedipal *or* pre-oedipal and regression is not *either* defensively motivated *or* a sign of early pathology. It is a matter of appropriate emphasis and analytic attention to the derivatives of developmental experiences as they enter into the analytic situation, oedipal *and* pre-oedipal, defensively motivated regression *and* regression to early pathology.

In chapters two and three we describe the analyses and follow-up experiences with two patients whose subsequent second analyses illuminated problems in separation-individuation that had not been adequately addressed. The first analyses focused on oedipal neuroses in an oedipal paradigm and resulted in significant intrapsychic changes and favorable consequences. The fact that the second analyses revealed and addressed earlier developmental problems does not detract from the significance of the interpretive efforts of the first analyses. If we do not impose unfortunate theoretical strictures before we look at the facts, outcome and follow-up research may permit us to integrate the theoretical and technical implications of our findings.

Our investigations also had their impact on our own

clinical work as analysts, and it is this clinical work that constitutes for us the best validation of our findings, serving to test these findings in the crucible of the analytic situation itself. For the clinical application of our findings we shall report some cases the management of which was significantly affected by our ongoing research, particularly in the termination phase. The cases can be formulated in a way that permits some integration of the ideas expressed earlier about the analytic alliance, the defense transference, and the transference neurosis, and that demonstrates some effects on technique. Our focus is on a more concentrated and carefully studied application of aspects of separation-individuation to tension regulation in the analytic process.

At the end of our clinical presentations, we shall survey the literature on follow-up studies with regard to method and content, and consider our findings in the context of that accumulating body of information.

In the theoretical sphere, we shall conclude with a developmental view of the analytic process at the level of clinical theory, proposing an elaboration of the analytic paradigm of symptom formation and a revision of the concept of defense transference. In effect, we focus attention on early developmental determinants of symptom formation and character structure. The classical formulation of symptom formation explains the development of structural conflict in terms of a core actual neurosis. In viewing this core phenomenon, the essential emphasis is on an economic imbalance, an intensity of affect and impulse that threatens to overwhelm the ego resources of the child. Neurotic symptom formation is an effort to avoid the repetition of a traumatic state. The theory of analytic therapy then holds that the recurrence of this traumatic state as the analysis unfolds is manageable by the patient because of his resources as an adult, magnified by the resolution of his conflicts in the analysis and the support of his analyst. The nature of that core traumatic state may, however, be conceptualized developmentally in more precise terms: that is, with regard to its genetic origins in the individual in specific deficits in tension regulation, deficits that are subject to analytic exploration and influence in any analysis.

The defense transference, as the characterological defensive organization evident at the onset of an analysis, serves as a shield against the transference neurosis and as an important coping mechanism of the ego in the face of conflict. In our revision, we view the defense transference as an outcome of the separation-individuation experience of the individual, guarding against the early conflicts for which it was a resolution and becoming a defense against oedipal conflict later in development.

Part I

Clinical Studies

Chapter 1

Assessment and Follow-Up in Psychoanalysis: The Method of Study

The initial step in our research was to devise a valid and reliable method of assessment of the results of analysis at termination and in follow-up studies. As clinicians and researchers we were convinced that there were compelling reasons, both practical and theoretical, for persisting in attempts to devise such a method in spite of the obvious complexities involved in any systematic effort to study the analytic process. Our experience has demonstrated the feasibility and usefulness of such an enterprise. We shall begin therefore by discussing the theoretical and clinical assumptions underlying our approach, describing our method of study and presenting an illustrative sample of the early results of our research.

The area of assessment of analysis at termination and in follow-up studies mobilizes in many analysts a defen-

This chapter originally appeared in slightly different form in the *Journal of the American Psychoanalytic Association,* 22: 542-567, 1974.

sive reaction about what has been achieved. Pfeffer (1959), in his follow-up studies, has observed and commented on a sensitivity about results on the part of training analysts, and even a frequent tendency to underestimate the effects of prolonged analytic efforts.

Such defensiveness and sensitivity may, of course, be explained on many grounds. It is our impression that they rest significantly on a confusion of assessment criteria in the face of complex data and a reactive effort to find global solutions and explanations of a grandiose nature. One solution to the problem may lie in turning to a more realistic and manageable assessment program that demonstrates a proper regard for the complexities and the special nature of the field of study.

Psychoanalysis as a treatment process has been most generally defined as the establishment of a therapeutic setting that permits the development of a transference neurosis, and the resolution of this transference neurosis by means of interpretation. The essential questions in assessment of the process are: What shall be used as criteria, and what is a suitable sample for study. Because the focus of the analytic process is on the reenactment of conflict and its resolution, the measurements must address themselves to observable changes in regard to conflict. When a patient presents himself for analysis, the deleterious effects of the repertoire of behaviors he has acquired for the management of conflicts are evident in his symptomatology and character—in the impoverishment, impairment, distortion, and unrealized potential of his ego resources. As the transference neurosis develops and is subjected to interpretations, changes in ego function are initiated. The freeing of energies bound in the defensive process and the working through of myriad derivatives of conflict result in changes that are demonstrable in specific ego functions and that are perceived clinically. Our measurements of change are therefore based on a study of ego functions as they enter into the analytic process at critical points.

APPROACH TO THE STUDY

A great deal of information of all kinds is gathered in the course of an analysis, and the problem is to reduce this complex data to a manageable level. To achieve this, it is necessary, as Wallerstein and Sampson (1971) have noted, to develop techniques that provide sufficient data for a particular purpose. For our purposes we have chosen to examine (1) the first few hours of the analysis, (2) the point in the analysis when termination was decided upon, (3) the last few hours of the analysis, and (4) four to six follow-up sessions, two to five years after termination.

The rationale for sampling the beginning and end of the analysis is self-evident. We have chosen to study the decision about termination as an intermediate point because it seemed probable that material at such a time would have the greatest potential for elucidating what analyst and patient regarded as critical in the process. The sampling of follow-up sessions two to five years after termination permits the research analyst to obtain a reading of the process and its consequences well after immediate reactions to termination.

Our criteria for assessing the clinical material rest firmly on a clinical base. In the course of the research, we have deliberately expanded the range of our criteria to incorporate new concepts such as the transformations of narcissism, the development of a cohesive self, and the stages of separation-individuation so as to permit the exploration of the analytic process in the context of a comprehensive developmental point of view. We have chosen as a scaffolding for the organization of the data (1) the nature of the alliance, (2) the special configuration of the Oedipus complex, (3) the defense transference, and (4) dreams.

The Nature of the Alliance

The first category, the nature of the alliance, is measured in terms of a scale of ego functions, ascending in complexity, that enter into the analytic alliance, and is essentially based on Zetzel's (1965a) developmental model. The first six items are a subgroup of ego functions regarded as prerequisites for the therapeutic alliance. They form the matrix of the analytic situation. The last eight items are more complex ego functions elaborated later in development and central to the analytic alliance. (A conceptualization of the analytic alliance in a developmental context is elaborated in Chapter 4.) They may exist as potentials at the beginning of an analysis, capable of development through the re-solution of conflicts in which they are involved. Although ego defenses are not specifically noted, they are, of course, assessed as they are implicated in other ego functions. Each of the items will be briefly described to convey a clearer impression of our intent in using them.

Basic trust refers to the capacity for relating to objects that results from a secure mother-child relationship in the earliest months of life. Basic trust is evident in sustained relationships and in a capacity for friendship, and its absence would be an element of paranoid psychotic phenomena. More circumscribed states of suspicion and mistrust may be evident in severe character problems.

Object constancy implies a cohesiveness and permanence of internal representations of objects, contributing to a tolerance for separation anxiety. It implies not only a mental representation of the object in its absence (a capacity identifiable at six to eight months), but also the psychological wherewithal to maintain object cathexis irrespective of frustration or satisfaction (identifiable at 18 to 27 months).

Self constancy. Based on investigations subsequent to the original report of our research, we have found it necessary to add a category, self constancy, as a parallel to object constancy in the assessment criteria. The assessment of self constancy requires an effort to gauge the cohesiveness and permanence of internal representations of the self.

Dyadic object relationship. The quality of object relationships reveals the degree of development that has occurred from the earliest states of symbiotic and transitional-object relationships (two to six months) through differentiation and individuation (six to 36 months). Separation-individuation marks the beginning of the dyadic relationship in the sense that the infant becomes capable of distinguishing himself from mother as a separate individual. Nurture and caretaking remain the prominent features of this stage. Thus, we would view sibling rivalry, which is presexual and involves competitive wishes for nurturing, in terms of a double dyad rather than a triadic relationship, even though there are three people involved.

Dyadic reality processing. The earliest form of reality processing, reality testing, refers to the capacity to distinguish between "mental representations stimulated by external, objective, manifest events and mental representations arising from internal events, memories, and fantasies" (Robbins and Sadow, 1974, p. 344). It is therefore contingent on self-object differentiation. In the context of a nurturing relationship with one object, the refinement and elaboration of the function of dyadic reality processing occurs with subsequent development of self- and object-representations and their interrelationships. Robbins and Sadow (1974) have elaborated a developmental hypothesis of reality functioning.

Tolerance of frustration, anxiety, and depression. The capacity to recognize and to some extent tolerate and contend with frustration, anxiety, and depression is a significant factor in any therapeutic alliance. The developmental line of anxiety as outlined by Freud (1926) extends from the threat of the loss of self in narcissistic disorders through the threat of the loss of the object, the threat of the loss of the love of the object, castration anxiety, and fear of an internalized conscience. The quality of anxiety in relation to the development of the ego ranges from traumatic intensity to signal anxiety. Zetzel (1965b) suggests a parallel developmental approach to the capacity to bear depression.

Triadic object relationship. This implies a cathexis of objects at an oedipal level, with an ability to relate sexually and competitively to two gender-differentiated objects.

Triadic reality processing. In the context of a triadic relationship, the function of reality processing is to differentiate the sexual and nurturing functions of the object. There is a resolution of a variety of distortions in the child's view of the sexual act, such as destructive or grandiose (narcissistic) fantasies of a pregenital nature, derived from earlier developmental stages. The primal scene fantasy serves as a paradigm in the study of triadic reality processing (Robbins and Sadow, 1974).

Potential for mastery of frustration, anxiety, and depression. We would expect that the capacity for mastery rather than simple tolerance would be enhanced in the process of analysis. The potential for mastery may be assessed at the outset by attention to the analysand's general problem-solving abilities and his response to initial interpretive efforts in the analytic situation. Any previous psychotherapy is, of course, a valuable source of data in this area.

Regression in the service of the ego. The capacity to regress and to utilize regression for self-observation and working through is an ego function essential to the analytic process. It may be assessed in relation to play and fantasy activity, sleep disturbances, reactions to illness, and responses in the analytic setting. No developmental line has been described with regard to this ego function.

Therapeutic split. In order to participate in the analytic process, the patient must be able to form a therapeutic split in the ego, by virtue of which he both experiences and observes his reactions. Such an ability rests on a previous capacity for introspection and self-awareness. It varies from hypercritical vigilance to a more ego-syntonic appreciation of and control over behavior, and includes elements of identification with parental attitudes. The self-observing function as it relates to experience has not yet been elaborated developmentally.

Self-analytic function. This capacity develops in identification with the analyst's analyzing function, combining self-observing and integrative functions. Studies such as those described in this book will help to clarify the development of such a function and to establish whether it endures beyond the analytic experience itself.

Self-soothing function. As a corollary to the assessment of the self-analytic function, we have added an assessment of the self-soothing function: the capacity to regulate tension that emerges as an outcome of the stages of separation-individuation. (This concept and category of assessment is further defined in Chapter 4, wherein we discuss the fate of the analytic alliance.)

Transformation of narcissism. Changes in this area

may be measured with regard to the development of empathy, humor, acceptance of the finiteness of life, creativity, and wisdom (Kohut, 1966), and would be reflected in the degree of self-constancy and the quality and integration of the ego ideal.

The analyst's contribution to the alliance is measurable as he describes his responses and interventions. Evidence of countertransference reactions and their fate is, of course, a part of the assessment.

Special Configuration of the Oedipus Complex

This category of assessment involves an effort to elucidate that unique organization of the patient's psychic contents that emerges developmentally from his solution to the oedipal situation. The analytic process has the potential to reopen this issue and subject it to possible re-solution. Regressive pregenital components are considered part of this special configuration. The sexual object choice, the response to sexual and competitive stimuli, the relationship to parents, siblings, and authorities are abiding patterns of responses, subject to scrutiny for evidence of change. While many of the elements entering into the assessment of the configuration of the Oedipus complex have already been examined in the categories of the analytic alliance, they are gathered together here, with oedipal conflict as the organizing focus of attention.

The Defense Transference

By this concept we refer to the characterological defensive organization of the patient, evident at the onset of an analysis and serving as a shield against the transference neurosis and as a major coping mechanism of the ego in the face of conflict. Defense transference has been discussed by Fenichel (1941) and described by Gitelson (1944). Although the term is not in common use, we regard the concept as a valuable one for personality assessment because the vicissitudes of the defense transference present an excellent index of change in the characterological armor. (A revision of this concept has evolved in the course of our work and the delineation and elaboration of it constitutes the final chapter of this book.)

Dreams

At each point in the analytic process dreams are subjected to careful investigation and serve as an indicator of change with reference to the nature of the conflict, the defenses employed, the solution arrived at, the nature of the transference, etc. French's (1954) investigation of focal conflict is the model for the effort to define the day-residue stimulus, the operative motives, and the solution of conflict.

METHOD OF STUDY

For some years, the Chicago Institute for Psychoanalysis has offered to advanced candidates a course in the assessment of completed analyses. Such a group of advanced candidates, together with the authors, constituted our research workshop. The analyst of a successfully completed case submitted a protocol presenting clinical material about the onset, decision to terminate, and final sessions of the analysis. This material was reviewed and studied microscopically by the group. This effort at analytic comprehension yielded ideas from a variety of perspectives, often significantly in conflict.

Rosen, in a panel on psychoanalytic research (Pfeffer, 1961a), reported on a study of gifted adolescents at the

New York Psychoanalytic Institute, innovative in that it used the continuous case seminar for investigative rather than didactic purposes and substituted group judgments for those of a single investigator. The advantages of this method, according to Rosen, lay in the large number of alternative propositions that were then subject to group criticism. Disadvantages were noted as well, such as dilution of responsibility, suggestibility, and a tendency to settle issues on the basis of authority or by parliamentary rules. These disadvantages were, however, rarely found to be operative. In our experience, discussion has been effective in clarifying what is idiosyncratic or inappropriate. And we would add that a far more important corrective measure for the possible disadvantages of group activity is provided when the group does not regard consensus as necessary. Where the evidence is contradictory or insufficient, alternative hypotheses may be recorded and reviewed in the light of subsequent data. Because the case is completed, the data is unaffected by the discussion. It is remarkable how broad and deep a view of the analytic process can be derived from such a discussion if one foregoes the need for consensus.

After a detailed and painstaking survey of the psychic apparatus as it is seen in the analytic process at three significant points, and the charting of results, the former patient becomes an ideal candidate for a follow-up study. The sample of clinical experience gathered in four to six follow-up interviews is roughly comparable in quantity to the material studied at each of the three points in the analytic process itself. Moreover, the follow-up material is particularly suitable to a study of the analytic process. Several patients seen in follow-up interviews essentially replicated the experience described in Pfeffer's (1959, 1961b, 1963) excellent studies. They demonstrated the revival of transference neurosis phenomena in the follow-up sessions, with a rapid subsidence that bore the marks of the prior analytic experience in the former patient's capacity to observe, report, analyze, and resolve his conflicts. This experience in miniature gathers together a remarkable harvest of data, raising and answering many questions about the analytic process and its aftermath.

In our method, the approach to the follow-up differed somewhat from that of the Pfeffer (1961b) study. It was decided that the follow-up analyst would participate in the assessment of the analytic process before doing the follow-up. This was a deliberate decision, made in order that the follow-up analyst would be able to acquire as much information as possible with which to confront the follow-up task. Our method of assessment, in which differences of opinion in the group are acknowledged and recorded, raises pertinent questions which can then be part of the informed interest of the follow-up analyst. There are obvious scientific objections to be raised about such an approach, inasmuch as the assessment procedure prior to the follow-up may create preformed judgments and expectations that modify the course of the follow-up sessions. In our opinion, however, the possible gain in presumed objectivity is purchased at too high a price scientifically. The fund of information, understanding, and informed questions created by the assessments permits the analyst to enter the follow-up situation fully aware of the unique research potential represented by the former analysand.

Once the assessment has been completed, the former patient is contacted with a frank request to participate in the follow-up research, the response to which has been uniformly positive to date. On the basis of 14 cases seen in follow-up, we can confirm Pfeffer's (1959) experience that the interviews have not had any apparent ill effects on the former patients. On the contrary, the opportunity to take a retrospective view of the analysis has appeared to be beneficial.

In the most general perspective, follow-up research may constitute the closest approximation to an experimental method we have developed in psychoanalysis. The entire analysis may be regarded as an experiment. Its repetition in the follow-up is an extraordinary opportunity for a second look. It is, in fact, a mini-analysis, shaped by the former patient's tendency to repeat his past experience in analysis. Yet the follow-up interviews also provide a sense of the ongoing nature of the process initiated in analysis. The researcher observes not a still photo at each assessment, but a panorama that changes as he looks at it and interacts with it. Transference neurosis potentials reappear in the follow-up interviews, and the former patient reveals successful solutions, uneasy compromises, and residual unresolved conflicts and transference in the repetition of the effort to master them. While the elements of repetition are noteworthy in themselves and provide a familiar context for the follow-up, it is the element of surprise that has made the project worthwhile. Our findings have indeed often surprised us and established new directions for our efforts, the results of which we shall elaborate in this monograph. In fact, one of the unanticipated aspects of the research is that some of the former patients studied have entered second analyses at later developmental crises in their lives and provided a further longitudinal view of psychopathology and the analytic process, confirming our tentative conclusions. We shall cite the evidence from this auxiliary source in its appropriate context.

Chapter 2

An Illustration of the Method of Study

In this chapter we shall present a case study from early in the project to illustrate our method. The patient studied has subsequently had a second analysis so that we have a recent follow-up of the follow-up. The case thus spans the time period of our research and may serve as a useful clinical introduction.

CASE 1

The patient was a 30-year-old white school counselor who began her analysis with a male analyst in March, 1966 and completed it in October, 1968 after 462 hours. The follow-up was conducted two years, nine months after termination. On entering treatment, her primary concern was her relationship with men, which included a preference for black men. Characteristically, she had a suc-

A portion of this chapter originally appeared in slightly different form in the *Journal of the American Psychoanalytic Association,* 22: 542-567, 1974.

cessful and enjoyable sexual relationship at the beginning, but she would then feel guilty, become very dependent, demanding, and resentful, the relationship ending in mutual frustration and antagonism. The patient described herself as insecure in her professional work, dissatisfied with herself, and as feeling unable to live up to her potential.

The patient's mother, a severe alcoholic, had always been dependent on her, making separations difficult; nor could the mother control her when she had temper tantrums as a child. When she was 16 or 17, her mother's chronic alcoholism became evident, and she was subsequently hospitalized several times. The patient had a sister, three years older, whom she regarded as more beautiful, more socially adept, and more successful academically, and whom she envied. She was also jealous of her brother, three years younger than herself. Her father was stable, and she had been "daddy's girl." Her parents were separated and reunited several times after she entered college, their divorce becoming final during the analysis.

In the first few years of school, the patient did poorly and had a speech problem that required treatment. In the sixth grade she related well with an admired teacher and subsequently became more interested and proficient in her academic performance. Her mother and older sister had both excelled in school and were experienced by her as difficult competitors. She completed high school and college with little difficulty, although she felt inferior to her sister, who had won many academic honors.

At age 20 she had two years of helpful and reassuring treatment with a social worker for depression and anxiety, precipitated by her mother's hospitalization for alcoholism. A little over a year prior to her analysis, she had had some 11 months of psychotherapy once weekly with a male analyst. He suggested analysis, and she sought help through the Institute Clinic.

It is clear that the task of communicating our various assessments and findings cannot be accomplished comprehensively within the confines of this chapter, no matter how much the material is condensed and abstracted. Perhaps it will be most useful if a representative sample of the assessments is offered, elucidating several categories. In this case we will follow the defense transference, the tolerance and mastery of depression, and the self-analytic function.

Defense Transference

As a characterological mainstay, the defense transference was repetitively enacted in the patient's relationships with men. After initial success in relating to them (including overt sexual gratification with black men), some guilt ensued, and there was a projection of a punitive mother imago onto her male partner, with an increasingly regressive nagging dependence and excessive demands. Her behavior usually elicited, first, "maternal" concern, then exasperation and eventual rejection. It protected her from internal oedipal conflict and was enacted whenever oedipal instinctual pressures were intensified.

In her psychotherapy prior to analysis, she had recapitulated her relationships with men in her relationship with her male therapist. An initial improvement was followed by increasing demands, mutual frustration, and an impasse. Her therapist recommended analysis.

Her anxieties were heightened when the first candidate to whom she was referred was put off by her behavior and rejected her. Regressive defense-transference phenomena were therefore in full bloom when she saw her eventual analyst. She was anxious and demanding, creating difficulties about the time of her visits, the lack of direction, and the use of the couch. The appeal for a mothering reaction and fear of a punitive mother were most evident. The analyst's responses were directed toward establishing a suitable matrix for an analytic effort. They consisted of conveying an empathic comprehension and tolerance of the patient's anxiety, encouragement in observing it, and, implicitly, providing hope that insight would make the anxiety more manageable for her. The projection of a hostile and critical mother imago onto the analyst was counteracted by interpretive efforts as well. In an early hour she pirouetted from the couch to the door after introducing a note of teasing seductiveness that softened the impact of her anxious demands and brought her oedipal conflict into view. Throughout the analysis, the defense transference appeared in unmodified form as a reaction to stress.

At the time of the decision to terminate, the defense transference was still very much in evidence. The patient alternately teased and complained. Hr complaints of being kicked out by a frustrating mother continued the idiom of the regressive defense transference against a backdrop of rising oedipal tension.

In the final hours of the analysis, the defense-transference motif was again quite clear. The patient expressed an irritating nagging dependence, with screaming and provocative behavior. It was striking that in these final hours the analyst's responses remained structuring and supportive and that the patient's screaming behavior had apparently not yielded to analysis, but remained an accompaniment of the active interpretive efforts. Although the patient revealed her curiosity about the analyst and his wife, she suppressed it without the development of analytic insight. A prominent teasing oedipal element was fused with her complaints and thereby acted out in the defense transference.

The follow-up interviews followed some significant changes in the patient's life, including her reactions to her mother's death and her marriage. They revealed profound post-analytic changes and an ongoing analytic process. She was cooperative and friendly. The patient herself readily handled a brief flare-up of hostility and complaint (about being examined and exposed to interpretations) with an amused and somewhat rueful contemplation of how difficult she had been in her analysis. While the considerable progress she had made on her oedipal problem, as well as on dyadic issues with her mother, was unmistakable, residuals of oedipal conflict were also evident. Because the initial arrangement was for four to six sessions, she assumed that the fifth session would be the last. Oedipal transference material had been mobilized in the discussion of her marriage, and she used the fifth hour to elaborate her preconscious awareness of some of the issues. An effort to deny oedipal concerns about her analyst with regard to the handling of her sexual feelings (by emphasizing dependency instead) dissolved into animated elaboration of those concerns in response to a quizzical look from the follow-up analyst. She accepted a final session in a most friendly manner, having recognized her wish to stop as similar to wishes to stop her analysis early because of her fear of talking about sexual feelings. In the final hour, however, she came 15 minutes late and although she participated in the conversation, it was apparent that she had sealed off her transference responses. She revealed that she had determined at the beginning of her analysis that she would finish in two to three years; her adherence to that timetable was a significant element in the defense transference. The follow-up reproduced this solution, although the defense transference was markedly reduced in its regressive features and the oedipal problem had been much alleviated in the interim.

Tolerance and Mastery of Depression

In discussing the separation-individuation process, Mahler (1972a) emphasizes that the differentiation of self and object, while concentrated in the period from the fourth or fifth to the 30th or 36th month of age, is never completed. Expressing her agreement with Erikson, she states: *"As is the case with any intrapsychic process, this one* [separation-individuation] *reverberates throughout the life cycle.* It is never finished; it can always become reactivated; new phases of the life cycle witness new derivatives of the earliest processes still at work" (p. 333). Such a theoretical outlook was the basis for Zetzel's (1965b) pioneering effort to set forth a developmental evaluation of depression, emphasizing the maturing capacity to tolerate and master depression as an ego function. This orientation seems particularly apt in looking at the tolerance and mastery of depression in the analytic process and its aftermath.

In the initial assessment, the capacity for tolerating depression and mourning was more potential than actual. Immediate regressive behavior when lying down on the couch and experiencing visual separation from the analyst was excessive. The weekend interruption, too, was an early problem in the analysis. The patient was, however, able to observe and report her experience with the reassuring structuring provided by the analyst.

When termination was discussed, the prospect of separation loomed large. Elements of negative maternal transference had been interpreted, and the patient reacted to her inability to perpetuate the squabbling with her mother in analysis (because of the analyst's interpretive stance) with depression. The need to give up such an old attachment was expressed in a brief dream in which "Mother passed on." It was following this that the patient pursued thoughts of termination. For some weeks prior to the setting of the date, she had recognized her avoidance of talking directly about termination and facing the depression she knew would be involved. Although she wept and became more demanding, she did set a termination date for herself. There followed, however, impulses to leave on a vacation to Canada to see her brother's family and their new baby, displacing her oedipal conflict from the analysis and wishing to leave rather than feel left.

The patient mentioned mourning and a recognition of her impending loss only in the last hour. She recognized a vengeful motive against her mother in her demanding and abusive behavior. As she put it, this leaving was not a relief, like leaving home had been, but a real loss. She nevertheless felt it was time to go. She cried in a more controlled fashion, acknowledged her gains in the analysis, and observed that she still had a lot of work to do, that she would try to work it out for herself and come back if she really needed to. Our assessment was that she had not really mourned the loss, but, in that final hour, had indicated that the preparations for a real mourning had been made.

Some four months after termination, the patient's mother died, after falling in an alcoholic stupor, precipitating intensive mourning. She had dreams of caring for her mother, and recognized how guilty she felt about wishes to take her father from her mother in the context of an affair with a married black man. She became involved in an intense relationship with a neurotic young white student whom she mothered as she mothered her own mother in her dreams, as a kind of expiation and vicarious experience of being mothered. She returned to see her analyst when she was considering marriage, and he helped to clarify her experience by pointing out the maternal significance of her boyfriend, cautioning her about marriage. Her mother's death, coming upon the heels of termination, intensified her quest for a solution. She was determined not to be like her mother in her self-destructiveness and her avoidance of closeness, but she also recognized the manner in which she had depreciated and vilified her mother and her analyst in the maternal transference. She accepted her identification with some of the more positive features of her mother, including wishes to be attractive, an interest in making clothes and decorating her home, a lively interest in books, and the pleasure in intellectual achievement that had character- ized her mother before the alcoholism became severe.

In the follow-up sessions, the solid nature of her achievement in the mastery of depression became quite evident. She described her reactions to the loss of her mother with appropriate affect and indicated that the positive identification with her mother was an enduring consequence of her analysis. She described her wedding ceremony, her tears at missing her mother's presence, and the even more poignant awareness that had her mother been present she could not have been all that the patient wanted. She seemed to have achieved a realistic view of her mother and the freedom to be like her mother in ways she regarded as admirable.

In the follow-up sessions, this achievement had its beneficial consequences in her relationship with the fol- low-up analyst. She sought direction and structuring in the first session, but when this was not forthcoming, read- ily grasped the opportunity for self-expression. This ap- peared to be indicative of a significant shift in defenses as a consequence of successful mourning, with a marked increase in her ability to cope.

It is interesting to note that the patient had not fully mourned the loss of her analyst. As she put it, she had not yet told him that she had finished her analysis. She referred to the fact that her last contact with her analyst had left the possibility of further consultation ambiguous and dependent on the results of her own efforts. It was arranged at the time that she would call and let him know the results of her efforts. But by the time of the follow-up interviews she had not called her analyst to inform him of her decision to proceed on her own or of her subsequent progress, although she did send him an announcement of the wedding.

Self-Analytic Function

The self-analytic function appears to combine a number of ego capacities and component identifications. Rangell (1970), in discussing the psychoanalytic process, states, "I put it that the psychoanalytic process is really the intrapsychic process under supervision. The patient's ego—every patient's ego, not only that of an analytic candidate—is being widened by the analytic process to become a better internal analyst. The ego of the patient, which is an internal analyst in life, learns to identify with the analyzing function of the analyst, not with his style, his mannerisms, his opinions, values, etc." (p. 197). Not only is there an identification with the analyzing function of the analyst, but those ego functions which have been developmentally impaired or stunted in the past are subject to possible correction.

The nature of the development of a self-analytic function in this patient is the third and last of the categories we shall elaborate. The initial assessment noted some positive factors in the patient's cognitive grasp of her therapeutic experience and a self-observing bent in remembering the content of preceding hours and thinking about them. There was, however, a need to use the process for reassurance, as described in the section on defense transference. The degree to which she could independently pursue an analytic task beyond self-observation was questionable.

When the termination date was set, the situation appeared unchanged. A structuring approach was clearly in evidence, and the patient acted out her regressive defense transference in her insistent demands and her reluctance to examine her own experience. Both the encouragement toward interpretive effort and the explanations were largely the analyst's.

At termination, self-observing capacities seemed good. The analyst's function again seemed disproportionate as he valiantly attempted to explain the patient's behavior. The final hour did include an expression of determination by the patient to proceed with the analytic work and a recognition that her understanding was incomplete. Self-analytic effort, however, was more a promise than an accomplishment.

In the follow-up interviews, further material appeared with regard to her self-analytic effort. She reported that following her analysis there were times when she would get into difficulties in relationships or in making a decision, and then would visit a friend and talk about her problem. She used a style of free association which helped her develop ideas and clarify her problem. She revealed that the permissive presence of another person remained a necessary ingredient in her efforts. She made no deliberate use of dreams, and expressed a self-depreciating evaluation of her own competence in understanding them. When her self-depreciation was brought to her attention, she acknowledged it but said that this was a pale reflection of what she had done before her analysis. Her description of her mourning made it clear that she had used dreams to capture a useful impression of how she felt, without deliberate analysis.

The most striking description of an unconscious process of integration was in regard to her marriage. She had always maintained a separation between affectionately friendly relations with men and sexual relations. After several months of a platonic relationship with her husband-to-be, she reacted jealously when a girlfriend developed a sexual interest in him. Her own sexual interest became evident to her. The relationship became more intense and sexual, and proceeded to a successful marriage. She described her husband as a stable, reliable accountant, whose qualities she would not have appreciated prior to her analysis, for she had always sought out men who were interesting because they needed help. She was not aware of any deliberate analytic effort connected with this relationship with her husband, yet she regarded it as a major accomplishment in her life, somehow made possible by her analysis.

In the follow-up sessions, her self-observing capacities appeared excellent. The deficit in her conscious integration of self-knowledge, while clearly much less than in the analytic process, remained a factor. The follow-up analyst again served to provide a permissive presence in which she could verbalize and organize information that seemed to be prestructured and ready to be tapped, requiring only an increment of approval to emerge. This integration of information was, however, not previously available to her in her solitary introspection.

Kramer (1959) has described the "autoanalytic function" as a spontaneous unconscious phenomenon directed toward the resolution of conflict on the basis of a complex process set in motion by the analysis itself. It may apparently be effective with or without conscious insight. In this case, the analyst's structuring activities and interpretations of negative maternal transferences were sufficient to permit the patient to tolerate the frustrations of the analytic process and its separations. The analysis prepared her to confront the task of mourning her mother's death and the loss of her analyst. Improvements in self-observation and the possibility of new integrations were a structural concomitant of this experience.

Miller, Isaacs, and Haggard (1965) have emphasized the significance of modifications in the whole range of self-object relations in the analytic process as it affects observation, the nature of communication, and the integrative capacity throughout an analysis. The self-analytic capacity develops through the resolution of conflict about independent functioning in all these areas. Its consolidation would appear, however, to rest on an identification with the analyst's analyzing function as an outcome of mourning, given that the loss of the analyst is a post-analytic development.

Follow-up of the Follow-up

The modifications in characterological defensive patterns, tolerance and mastery of depression, and self-analytic functions documented in the above account rested significantly on the structuring activities of the analyst, in whose persuasive and benign presence the patient could manage her potential for irritating, nagging dependence accompanied by screaming, provocative behavior. A further contact with the patient revealed that she was undergoing a second analysis which had already yielded some striking insights into her characterological defenses.

Eighteen months after the follow-up, she returned to her treating analyst for consultation and subsequently resumed analysis with another analyst in the graduate clinic. In the course of her first pregnancy, which took place during this 18-month interim, her father died. He had sustained an illness that made his usual independent, self-reliant, and authoritarian behavior quite impossible. The emotional upheaval he experienced was a burden for the patient and a complication of her pregnancy. Her own emotional turmoil convinced her of the need for further analysis. She accepted her husband's kind and attentive behavior gratefully but tearfully and reported that she had lost several gifts he had given her, including two watches and her engagement ring. She recognized this as symptomatic behavior since it was quite unlike her to lose things. Sexual activity was infrequent, about every three or four weeks, and associated with dreams in which she pictured herself in a masochistic role, being held down and mounted. Her husband's hesitant approach and desire for her to initiate sex was much at odds with her fantasies. At the time she actually resumed her analysis she was chiefly preoccupied with a problem with her daughter who was then six months old. She had breastfed the baby and had had difficulty weaning her. She recognized in the effort at weaning a developing conflict about setting limits altogether.

Her behavior starting the second analysis surprised her analyst because she seemed quite untutored in her role as an analysand. She couldn't be comfortable on the couch and couldn't free associate. She displayed eruptions of affect and giggliness. The screaming and demanding behavior noted in her first analysis was now accompanied by baby talk. The analyst attempted to confront and question her behavior rather than control and structure it. Her wishes to be controlled, led, and directed were focused on as a problem. For the first six to nine months, the analytic alliance remained tenuous. A breakthrough occurred when her behavior was identified as a repetition of early childhood experience. She had had eczema as an infant and had been restrained with cloths tied to the bedposts from earliest infancy until she was two-and-a-half or three years old, in order to prevent her desperate scratching. Derivatives of this interaction with her mother were skeletal elements in her personality. An overcontrolling, constricting environment was what she sought out as an external set of limits to control rising tensions of whatever variety. In retrospect, she recognized that she had been unable in her first analysis to experience a genuine common goal or purpose with her analyst. Although she appreciated his conscientious labors and believed that he had been helpful, their affective interchanges were muted and there was no sense of intimacy. The insights gained had a superficial and even programmed quality for her. She recalled that she had entered her first analysis with a fixed period in mind for its duration and this too had served as an external limit on her involvement.

With the recovery of memories and fantasies about the eczema experience and their working through, the nature of the analytic alliance changed, no longer requiring structuring activity from the analyst. The patient's self-analytic capacity, deepened by insight into the roots of her infantile screaming and demanding behavior, increasingly recognized and mastered instances in which rising tensions elicited such nascent responses. The patient's memory for previous sessions improved as did her ability to associate and provide good observational material. She experienced and expressed curiosity about her analyst, wishes for an exclusive relationship with him, and sexual dreams with clear transference referents. A derivative of the need for external controls of her affects was introduced by her decision to have a second child about a year into her analysis. The decision was rationalized on the grounds of her advancing age but also served to gratify her oedipal fantasies in that she would not have to tolerate the full intensity of her frustration and her masochistic fantasies. Her solution was itself more happily adaptive as a form of acting out than in the past and it was, of course, the object of analytic scrutiny.

This case provides a dramatic illustration of the significance of early developmental experiences in a dyadic context in establishing characterological patterns of reaction to stress and symptomatic behavior. Such patterns do not simply involve defensive reactions against oedipal conflicts. They require analytic exploration with regard to tension regulation in separation-individuation experiences as well. The developmental crisis that this patient faced in bearing a child and losing the support of her father reawakened in an acute form her problems with tension regulation. Setting limits for her child was an impossible task that brought her back for a second analysis. The structuring activities and benign presence of her first analyst had served as a patch on these early problems as he focused on oedipal conflicts. The positive accomplishments of the first analysis were documented but subject to disruption in the face of renewed stress in an aspect of the patient's life and the analytic relationship that had not been analyzed.

This case serves to highlight a rather consistent finding that emerged in our studies, one that we shall be amplifying throughout this book: namely, a relative neglect by analysts of early developmental determinants as they enter into the analytic process.

Chapter 3

The Fate of the Transference Neurosis: Recurrent Patterns of Conflict and Changes in Ego Functions

In any study of a psychoanalysis, intrapsychic conflict and its resolution is a natural object of inquiry. The psychoanalytic situation, by definition, facilitates the development of a transference neurosis which, in derivative form, captures the essence of infantile conflicts that have made themselves evident in neurotic symptomatology. Interpretive efforts are directed toward the resolution of these conflicts through insight into their genetic origins and repetitions in the transference. What is the outcome of this activity? In this chapter, we shall describe our position with regard to clinical theory and present a case study of a successful analysis and its follow-up to illus-

    A portion of this chapter originally appeared in slightly different form in the *Journal of the American Psychoanalytic Association,* 23: 761-782, 1975.

trate our research findings and elucidate our current hypothesis about the fate of the transference neurosis.

In studying the psychoanalytic process, French (1958) described recurrent psychodynamic cycles, explaining them as based on the persistence and repetition of integrative patterns as conflicts are activated. He wrote:

> From the point of view of the integrative mechanism as a whole we can distinguish two kinds of problems. (1) Primary problems in adjustment to external reality and (2) Secondary problems concerned with mastery of internal pressures. This distinction . . . gives us another criterion by which we can recognize a patient's successive neurotic cycles. Each cycle begins with a primary problem and continues then with problems of internal mastery until the activated pressures are discharged [pp. 115-116].

French's concept of recurrent dynamic cycles based on the remobilization of conflicts along with their instinctual roots and ego solutions appears quite consistent with the findings of follow-up studies. Seitz (1968) has emphasized the potential usefulness of the cycles in analysis as a research tool with which to study the course of the analysis. Recurring phenomena, if they can be defined, are clearly subject to comparison for evidence of change.

The cyclic nature of psychological phenomena provides the rationale for the method of assessment we have described, in which samples of clinical material are viewed at critical points in the analysis—the initial interviews, the decision to terminate, the termination interviews—and in follow-up interviews. At each of these times, one may reasonably expect a level of stimulation that would mobilize conflict and challenge and reveal the ego resources and coping mechanisms of the individual.

We shall now describe a supervised analysis of a hysterical character neurosis. As noted above, our study of the process involves a careful examination of the range of ego functions implicated in the analytic alliance, the defense transference, dreams, and the special configuration of the Oedipus complex. We shall present a selective sample of our assessment in order to illustrate the recurrent patterns of conflict and the development of a self-analytic function as critical features of the analytic process.

CASE 2

The patient entered analysis at the age of 25, when she was about to be graduated from a professional school. She had been involved in an episodically exciting but essentially stagnant and self-destructive relationship with a man for five years, during which time her dreams of marriage and children had been frustrated. She suffered recurrently from feelings of depression and worthlessness, and she attributed these feelings to her tendency to submit to frustrating relationships of this type. She also described some difficulty in her work. In fact, she had been referred for analysis by a woman supervisor with whom she had had some difficulty.

She grew up in a close-knit family as the younger of two children; her brother was a year and a half older. She had always enjoyed a close relationship with her father—a successful philosopher—based on open discussions of philosophy and religion. He was always supportive and logical. She admired his liberal views and his scholarship. Her mother was more exciting and volatile, at times domineering and intrusive. She regarded her mother, who suffered from chronic somatic diseases which made her cross, irritable, and demanding, as even more brilliant than her father. Mother frequently worked on her father's papers and was heavily involved in organizational activities in the community. Her relationship with her mother was characterized by a good deal of fighting as well as periods of affection. Her mother showed a marked preference for her brother, who was a brilliant student, a young prodigy. She always felt intellectually inferior to him, but proudly recalled her physical superiority in fighting his battles for him as a youngster. When he was 13, he was discovered to have a chronic debilitating disease. He achieved great success in school, but never fulfilled his promise, changing colleges and career choices several times.

Her father moved the family twice in connection with career opportunities when the patient was five and 18. She grew up with a contempt and aversion for illness and dependence, in reaction to the problems of her mother and brother. Her early sexual interests occasioned anxiety. The patient and her brother had had a close relationship marked by some sexual interest, much of which the patient had repressed. Her mother always worried that she would be too giving, and cautioned her about the danger of being victimized. She was drawn to inferior boys who were not very acceptable to her family. In her early description of her problems, she recalled her first menstrual period. She didn't want her father to know, but she remembered excitedly coming down the stairs and her father saying, "I hear you're a young woman." It made her nervous. While her relationship with her father was largely intellectual, she experienced some of his behavior as seductive.

When she was in her senior year in college, her mother required surgery and was bedridden and helpless for several months. The patient devoted herself to the almost constant physical care of her mother. She was angered by her mother's demands and bitter outcries, and she experienced disgust and shame when she had to attend to her mother's bodily needs. On one occasion during her mother's rehabilitation, she accompanied her father to a professional meeting in another city. They slept in rooms separated by a partition, and the patient suffered an anxiety attack. It was at the time of her mother's illness that she began to date her boyfriend more seriously and had intercourse for the first time. At about the same time, her brother, now in a distant city, divorced his first wife and began to deteriorate mentally and physically, sporadically taking drugs and essentially being supported by his parents.

Opening Phase of Analysis

In the opening phase of her analysis, the first cycle of her conflicts ran its course in 33 sessions. In the second interview she displayed her characteristic mode of defense. She was brusque, curt, disdainful, and expressed disappointment at and criticism of the analyst's youth and inexperience. He was initially discomfited, but recognized the behavior as defensive, a phallic-aggressive defense transference that protected her from her conflicts. His acceptance of her and his recommendation of analysis drew a response of initial pleasure and then, as she felt threatened by the gratification, a barrage of questions and objections. She was able to recognize a pattern of such behavior with some relief and proceeded, after four sessions, with the first couch hour.

With the breach in her characterological armor, concerns about pleasing her mother immediately became apparent. The initial impact of the analytic process resulted in a missed second couch hour, ostensibly because she had a cold. On the following day she reported a pair of dreams which she had had during the day of her illness.

In the first dream she was supposed to meet her girlfriend and live with her, but someone said they would have to meet at the Upper Avenue National Bank. It felt like a long walk from her present home. In the light of the material that subsequently emerged in the analysis, this dream may be viewed as an expression of conflict over homosexual wishes, the conflict itself serving a regressive defensive function in distancing the patient from a more troubling conflict over heterosexuality. The obvious parallel in the dream to the missed couch hour expresses the regressive and distancing homosexual transference that subsequently became more clearly evident in the analysis. In the second dream the patient was locked in the bathtub and there were a "whole mess" of crabs and oysters which were disgusting to look at. Again in the light of the subsequent material, and the first dream itself, this dream may be viewed as an expression of conflict over heterosexual impulses, with the crabs and oysters—the "disgusting mess"—symbolizing those impulses. It is noteworthy that heterosexual interests were conspicuous by their absence in her associations to this dream. Her position in the bathtub again suggests a parallel to the analytic situation, as a transformation in the dream state of her newly assumed position on the couch.

The regressive theme unfolded in the context of issues of nurturing rooted in her early dyadic relationship with her mother. She was critical of her perfectionistic and demanding mother, grudgingly admired her brilliance and ability, and depreciated her for her illness. Many of her associations related to her wishes to be appreciated by women, including women supervisors and roommates. A common complaint was about her mother's preoccupation with her brother. In the analytic situation she maintained a businesslike narrative style, analyzing her family and reflecting on their motives. In the regressive homosexual transference she viewed the analyst as critical and perfectionistic, fearing that he would comment about her being resistant or silly. Occasionally she would smile furtively at the analyst on the way to the couch and refer to her mixed feelings of anticipation and anxiety about coming to sessions.

In hour 26 she reported that in her father's absence her mother had invited her to sleep in her bedroom for company because she had received an anonymous phone call and was frightened. She refused because it felt too close. She recognized an exaggerated annoyance and embarrassment in the presence of her mother, cringing at her touch. This reaction took on a pronounced transference coloring when she reacted to the analyst's cough as she had to her mother's and acknowledged similar feelings of embarrassment in the session. Her irritability and contentious manner were interpreted as reactive to her embarrassment, and she enthusiastically associated that she acted tough and tomboyish to keep people from seeing a softer part of herself.

With the focus shifting to softer, more feminine feelings, heterosexual feelings emerged in conjunction with a view of her mother as a more admirable person. She reported the following dream in the 33rd hour:

> I don't know who the person I was with was, but I felt sexually stimulated and had an orgasm, and then my body started to move seductively into a ballet. I had a male partner. I felt a little awkward, dancing like a puppet on a string. Next thing I was in a house. There was a big bedroom with plush Hollywood-like purple cushions. I was on a motorcycle which I didn't think I knew how to ride, but I whipped it into a high gear, weaved through various rooms under overhanging bras and panties and into a room where my mother and brother were sitting. My brother's head was on her lap

and she was kissing him more like a lover. My mother
called me over to tell me something she was telling him
but to me it didn't look like they were talking at all.

She associated to the anxiety attack she had had three
years earlier when she had accompanied her father to his
meeting, speculated about her attachment to him, and in
the end questioned her flip attitude about her mother and
brother, wondering if their relationship didn't stir up
more jealousy than she thought. The dream had of course
ended with a primal scene displaced onto her mother and
brother.

The pattern of conflicts in this opening phase may be
briefly highlighted. It was initiated by a favorable interpretive breach in the defense transference and the
stimulation afforded by acceptance for analysis. The repetitive patterns of conflict discernible in later analytic
material confirmed our inference that heterosexual conflict was triggered by the onset of the analysis. Homosexual conflicts appeared more clearly in this initial
material as a regressive defense against heterosexual
wishes, the regression proceeding to a nurturing dyadic
level at which the patient described her rivalry with her
brother. Softer feminine feelings emerged as she recognized her fear and disgust at physical closeness with her
mother and described a tomboyish defensive reaction.
Heterosexual conflict was then more explicit in the third
dream. In this first cycle of conflict the homosexual
regression and distancing defense of the first two dreams
remained apparent in the third. Her heterosexual feelings were defended by tomboyish behavior, but had advanced from an early disguised and symbolic interest to
a more explicit, more sharply focused representation of
oedipal conflict.

Decision about Termination

Around the end of the third year of her analysis the patient began an intense affair with a recently divorced man. Although the affair began in the midst of an oedipal transference, another cycle was set in motion as regressive pregenital wishes and fears emerged. She recognized intense homosexual longings in the transference over the next few months after discovering blatant bisexual trends in her lover. She elaborated on her rivalry with her brother and her deepest yearnings for her mother. In her rivalry with her brother and her deepest yearnings for her mother she acknowledged and worked through her homosexual interests in the transference. The defensive aspect of her homosexual interests then became clear. She recognized that she had chosen weak, mothering men, who were not quite men, to avoid further confrontation with her sexual feelings about her father. In reaction to this insight she terminated a relationship in which she had enacted her defensive use of a weak man with mutual frustration and unhappiness. Her wish for a relationship with a strong man was experienced and elaborated in the transference resulting in a sense of accomplishment. She then raised the possibility of termination of her analysis in a year.

There was a fractionated approach to the decision about termination characteristic of the patient's tendency to withdraw and act out. The recurring discussion about a date for termination had some of the quality of subtle fighting observed in the early material. Although there were no missed appointments, she did leave one stormy session five minutes early.

A surge of genital sexual feelings for the analyst had caused her to experience the continuation of the analysis—by his not fixing a termination date—as a seduction similar to her father's behavior in the past in leaving the door to the bathroom open. As the cycle of conflict was repeated, sexual elements in the defensive homosexual context, which had regressively sexualized the nurturing experience with her mother, became explicit and differentiated. The nurturing issues were particularly evident in this patient's reaction to the death of the woman who headed her agency. She recognized feelings of liberation, in spite of guilt that her progress was at the expense of another woman, who represented mother. The patient nevertheless continued to demonstrate a capacity to view her mother and herself in more realistic terms. She could discern her mother's softness and nurturing qualities even as she continued to see some of her behavior as devilish. Guilt and reaction formations in response to her anger at and envy of her brother were elaborated.

Her recognition of the "wrong" things she had sought from men as maternal substitutes resulted in an interest in finding a strong man. Positive oedipal feelings were clearly focused. The patient grew sick to her stomach when she learned her analyst had children. She experienced open wishes for a baby. After an effort to recreate a special feeling with her analyst such as she had had with her father, she described her disillusionment and anger. She experienced intense bitterness about the lack of consummation in the transference. In her relationship with her parents, she described a happier identification with her mother, an ability to compete with her, and some success in differentiating them currently from her infantile objects.

The stepped-up pace with which the patient's patterns of conflict repeated themselves in the period of the decision to terminate suggested her greater tolerance for anxiety and depression. The experiential quality of the material indicated a mobilization of the transference neurosis in considerable intensity. Latent material of the initial experience of conflicts was more manifest. The themes were more elaborated in consciousness and associated with higher ego functioning.

Termination

In the last few sessions, the recurrent pattern of conflict was again apparent in response to the impending separation. In fact, an entire cycle of conflict was discernible within a single session. The patient had decided to leave her job and her analysis simultaneously, arousing some anxiety in her analyst about whether termination should not be postponed. The analyst's anxiety was experienced as seduction, and stimulated regressive conflict. The patient described her difficulty in giving up a woman friend at work. Again she briefly pursued her feelings of jealousy about her mother's attention to her brother. She acknowledged her wish to push her brother out, recalling an old dream in which she had one scoop of ice cream and wanted two.

In an essentially positive exchange, the analyst described the analysis as a pretty good one, whereupon the patient took a few nips at him as a fledgling analyst. There seemed to be a residual projective element in her feeling that the analyst was not satisfied with her and would still want to help her. Her own view of the analysis as "damned successful" and her comments about her analyst may have been partly legitimate, but also hearkened back to the defense transference attitude of disdainful criticism. Still, in these last few hours, she acknowledged that she didn't have all the answers and that there was work left to be done to modify her phallic-aggressive stance. Its reappearance as a defense here was in modified form, both in intensity and in duration, and was followed by the reemergence of heterosexual wishes.

She reexperienced aspects of her oedipal conflict, demonstrating in the clinical material a capacity for selective identification with her mother. She could choose what she wanted to do without being limited by her mother's preferences. She could disagree without getting into a battle. She expressed the desire for an exchange of gifts with her analyst as a way of terminating the relationship and in this context, her desire for a baby as a gift from the analyst became quite explicit. She described sequential wishes for a penis inside her and for a strong man who would impregnate her. She was aware of a complex of feelings in relation to sexuality, including wishes to be held and touched. In her associations and thoughts, she was able to differentiate parents and analyst as incestuous objects from the real men in her life who were like them. Her description of her wishes was finely tuned, even poetic.

In one hour she elaborated her wishes for a man and a gift (baby) with associations to her having had some instrumentation around her vagina as a little girl in the doctor's office. Her impressions of the visit were vague. Her associations involved both a threat of injury, as though she had suffered a mutilating castration as punishment for her jealous castrating impulses toward her brother and fantasies of being impregnated, which she acknowledged as an active preoccupation in the transference. The following session she reported a dream. "I had a dream last night. A young woman was sort of dancing, and during her dance she lifted her blouse and displayed her breasts. But it was done in a very natural way. Breasts? Are they for a baby? Why breasts? Why not other female parts? But there was a feeling that I have accepted my whole body. There was a free-spirit feeling." The analyst asked if anyone was watching, to which the patient replied that there was a man, perhaps the analyst or her father, that the dance was done twice, and perhaps more of her body was shown. The dream displayed the familiar distancing defense in response to the issue of heterosexuality. The breasts seemed to have implicit dyadic significance rooted in the mother-child relationship. The audience for her exhibitionism was left ambiguous until the analyst raised the question. She reported that the dance was done twice, and perhaps the genitalia were part of her body image in the initially suppressed second dance. Heterosexual interests were not explicit in the manifest dream. But in her question as to why only the breasts had appeared, the patient seemed to have acknowledged directly the suppressed heterosexual interest. Once again the entire pattern of conflict had been repeated and was being worked through at termination.

Follow-Up

Six follow-up interviews were conducted at weekly intervals two years and nine months after termination of the analysis. The interval had been crowded with both happy and tragic events with which the patient had coped successfully. Some ten months after completion of her analysis she was married. Her husband's mother collapsed a month later with serious physical problems, and survived only as a chronic invalid. Some 18 months after completion of her analysis her mother died, and two months later her brother died. Her father had remarried about a year after her mother's death.

In response to our inquiry explaining the research, the patient expressed an enthusiastic interest in participating in the follow-up study. Having indicated her interest, she pressed for some early appointments in a manner reminiscent of her aggressive defense transference stance. The interviews were held as originally scheduled. She reported that she and her husband were about to purchase and move into a new house and that she was six weeks pregnant. Her call to start the interviews at an earlier date had coincided with the beginning of her pregnancy. In the first interview she reported the chronology of events since termination. She described her happy marriage to a successful and understanding professional man whom she had met in the months following the termination of her analysis. She had found a suitable job in her field, and although there were initial problems with rebelliousness about rules and regulations, she had created in the ensuing months a productive and rewarding career for herself. Her pregnancy was planned and much desired, and in its early weeks, accompanied by the happy excitement of purchasing a new house and car.

The repetitive pattern of conflicts described earlier recurred quite clearly in the follow-up. In effect, there were two cycles within the six sessions. The flurry of defense transference at the start of the follow-up has already been described and its coincidence with the onset of her pregnancy noted. In describing the deaths in her family, the patient was appropriately depressed and near tears. The deaths of her mother and brother had reawakened familiar dyadic problems. Some turmoil at work had occurred, but she had been able to see her part in the troubles. Her husband's support, comfort, and approval were quite important to her. Her mastery of depression involved a striking sublimation in helping others confronted with similar situations. A trace of the argumentativeness that her analyst had noted appeared in her response to the follow-up analyst's questioning of a slip she had made about the date of termination of her analysis—there was some confusion about the year in which she had finished. She recalled with considerable annoyance her feelings that her analyst had wanted to hang on to her and to continue the analysis and that he hadn't appreciated her accomplishments. Toward the end of the first interview, the follow-up analyst responded to the increasing nurturing demands implicit in the content with a reminder that there were six follow-up sessions altogether.

At the beginning of the second session, she noted querulously that she was a minute or two late only by the follow-up analyst's clock because she had stopped to give an old woman friend a capsule summary of developments in her life. It was reminiscent of the homosexual defense in the first dream of her analysis after the missed hour.

She acknowledged a sensitivity about feeling dependent, describing her lifelong interest in independent functioning and an intolerance in latency for being cared for. She described as well a concern about being evaluated, which had been particularly disruptive with women supervisors in the job she had quit at the end of her analysis. As the second follow-up interview drew to a close, she experienced a negative maternal transference reaction to the follow-up analyst, questioning him irritably as to whether she would receive any feedback. She recalled that her own analyst had listened for four sessions before advising analysis. The follow-up analyst then asked whether she feared a repetition of that experience, and she acknowledged her anxiety about evaluation. But when the follow-up analyst then questioned the appropriateness of this anxiety in the face of the very impressive gains in her life, she calmed down perceptibly and agreed to talk about it further the next time.

In the third interview she indicated that she had had a very positive response to the intervention at the end of the session. She mentioned that she had recognized the patient immediately before her as a man she had briefly dated some ten years earlier and compared the kind of solicitude of this man's father, a busy and prominent person, with the ineptitude of his son. The shift to an oedipal setting was thereby signaled. She described her initial concern about getting pregnant because it had taken her mother many years to accomplish it, although she had herself succeeded in three months. She elaborated her fears that she would find herself in the same position as her mother with problems about socializing or raising children. She was pleased that she had been finding the company of women gratifying, although her interest was still in doing the major things with her husband and being with him when he was available. She felt that she had broken free of her mother's pattern of acting like a martyr. Yet she experienced fears about her father's death and her husband's death. Her mother and brother had died abruptly, and it was hard to be the survivor. When the possibility of a guilt reaction was raised with her, she thought it had more to do with guilt about her brother's sad demise after his brilliant promise. She regretted tearfully that her mother would not be around to knit for the baby and that she had had no opportunity at all for a reconciliation with her brother before he died, as she had had with her mother.

The cycle of conflict was apparent in a keynote of defense transference behavior: a homosexual regression with dyadic components and a distancing defense, followed by the cathexis of a positive oedipal situation overlaid with guilt concerning the deaths in her family. It is interesting to note that at the end of the third interview, she mentioned that she had arranged some business matters with her husband so that she would be able to keep her fourth appointment. Her husband would wait for her in the library and meet her in the waiting room after the interview. The arrangement was realistic enough, but one could also infer that the husband had been introduced into the situation as a protective figure in response to intensified transference feelings.

In the fourth interview a second cycle of conflict began. The closing of the purchase of her house had occurred in the interim. Her dress, which had been sophisticated in the preceding sessions, was now schoolgirlish. She looked pleased but somewhat overwhelmed as she talked about the house. She had a headache. With a sudden shift in topic and manner, she turned to the follow-up research and fired a series of questions at the follow-up analyst about its purpose, organization, criteria for evaluation, wondering whether a board of analysts would not be better than a single analyst and expressing concern about the experience of the follow-up analyst. It was sharply reminiscent of her reactions to her original analyst in the defense transference. Since her questions reflected an understandable curiosity, they were answered. At the same time, her anxiety about evaluation was brought back into focus.

She acknowledged her anxiety and returned with a sigh to her headache and tension. She was afraid that something bad would happen in the face of all her happiness and good fortune. She said that since the death of her mother and brother there were times when she had been unable to enjoy sex, although sex had been very good at other times—as when she got pregnant. Her thoughts focused on her mother's coming back to haunt her about sex. In the fifth interview she reviewed with tears her mother's terminal illness and acknowledged some guilt about resenting her mother's bitter demands and feeling she had surpassed her mother in some ways. More poignantly, after an empathic response from the follow-up analyst, she returned to the dyadic context, describing her acute awareness of her jealousy and competition with her brother, her fury at feeling unappreciated, and her feelings of anger, and guilt about her brother's death. With defensiveness reduced to a minimum, there was an intense and deeply experienced expression of mourning and a wish for reconciliation in a dyadic nurturing context. At the end of the fifth session she asked with evident regret whether the sixth session was the last. The follow-up analyst began to wonder about the policy of limiting the follow-up sessions to a fixed number. With the possibility of an extension in mind, he recalled the nature of her termination, when she had questioned whether her analyst would let her go. Once again there was the question of the paternal transference, whether the door to a seductive interplay was open or closed. Even in these details, the repetition of the analysis proceeded.

In the final session she appeared casual and smiling and reported feeling that all the things she had said to the follow-up analyst she had said before. She has been reworking things since her mother and brother died. She'd have to wait and see what the effect of these interviews would be. She reported with a wide grin several dreams she had had. In one, her stepmother had appeared to be taking care of her mother. Or was it that her mother and stepmother were together and her father was taking care of both of them? In the dream it was all right with her. She could accept both of them. The second dream was about the follow-up analyst. The analyst walked out with the guy that preceded her and told her that he could not see her, but had to go to a meeting. She was angry. She had come all this way and would not be seen. In the dream, the analyst suggested that she return the following week for an interview.

She recognized that she was reacting to the last session as a kind of termination and that the dream meant to her that she didn't want to terminate and was postponing it. After a querulous response to a question about the analyst's leaving with the patient who preceded her and an expression of dissatisfaction about the results of dream analysis, she recalled, in association, the early dream of her analysis involving her mother and brother and her tearing around the place on a motorcycle. She was competing with her brother for her mother's attention. She laughingly recalled that at one time she had been a tomboy and acknowledged her competitive feelings with the follow-up analyst's patient.

The dream about her mother's return had in it a note of continued conflict about oedipal wishes, with a continued distancing defense against heterosexuality. She had expressed the wish that her analyst might learn of her pregnancy through the follow-up, although in other instances she had written him and had even visited him once after her brother's death. That particular communication seemed conflicted. As she described the purchase of maternity clothes and preparations for the birth of her baby, she seemed to glow with pleasure. Her parting comments were an expression of pleasure about the follow-up interviews (which the follow-up analyst shared) and a request that she be informed if her case were included in a paper on the follow-up research. We might infer from the juxtaposition of this request with the description of the birth preparations immediately preceding it that the future paper symbolized the wished-for gift that had been so closely identified with the patient's wish for a baby at the end of her analysis. Her request was also a reaction to termination, expressing a wish for an ongoing relationship.

Self-Analytic Function

This case study demonstrates the persistence of recurrent patterns of conflicts. It is our hypothesis that such recurrent patterns are childhood acquisitions and, as such, relatively immutable. They are the unique outcome of the maturational and developmental influences shaping an individual's early experience and are intrinsic to the organization of the infantile neurosis. Our follow-up studies to date support this hypothesis. The effect of analysis is not the obliteration of conflict, but an increased potential for tolerance and mastery of frustration, anxiety, and depression through the development of a self-analytic function. As a preconscious coping mechanism, it develops in identification with the analyst's efforts to observe, understand, and integrate psychological events. Originating in the therapeutic split, it may be assessed by careful attention to the experience of the patient in the analytic process. Refinements in empathy, self-observation, object relations, reality processing, communication, and integrative skills are significant to the development of the self-analytic function. To illustrate this thesis, we shall briefly discuss the nature of the changes observable in this case as they are illustrated by the follow-up material.

The follow-up experience demonstrated an ongoing process in which the resources developed in the analysis were turned to reworking internal stimuli and coping effectively with the demands of reality. Marriage, mourning the death of her brother and mother, problems with supervision at work, and pregnancy provided a high level of stimulation in the less than three years since the completion of her analysis. These stimuli had had their impact in the framework of familiar cycles of conflict, albeit outside a formal analytic context, and had tested the patient's ego resources. The repetition of the cycles in the follow-up provided a view of their current intrapsychic status.

The evidence for a continuing self-analytic function in the follow-up may readily be delineated. The patient recalled her own description of a fear of dependence at termination of her analysis, and questioned it in the follow-up, elaborating some of the genetic factors. Her mourning intensified her concerns in a dyadic context and influenced her handling of anxiety. She described this process quite clearly. In a regressive fashion she would have a temper tantrum with her husband, then feel dissatisfied with herself for not being able to exercise more control. These reactions appeared to be part of her active mourning. Following such regressive outbursts she would recover and think about her experiences and talk to her husband about them. The understanding she developed was thus the result of her own effort. In the follow-up she ambivalently acknowledged her guilt about being the survivor as it entered into fears that she would suffer her mother's tragic fate. In her sexual anxiety reactions she herself recognized that her reactions were worst on the anniversary of her mother's death, when she was ovulating and wanted to be pregnant. She thought that to enjoy sex was to dishonor her mother, and she had had some concerns about being hurt and torn up. She recognized that her fears were related to being haunted by her mother and described her own impression that she was reworking what she had learned in her analysis as she struggled with her mourning. In reporting her dreams in the final session of the follow-up, she denied her competence at understanding dreams and then proceeded to interpret effectively her reactions to the last session as a termination experience, recalling an early dream in her analysis and recognizing the connections between jealousy of her brother and jealousy of the follow-up analyst's male patient.

In contrast to her reaction to termination in her analysis, where she had projected her wish to continue onto her analyst, in the follow-up she acknowledged it as a wish of her own. Her positive oedipal feelings could be inferred from her experience in the final session but were not as available to her consciousness as the dyadic wish to continue the sessions. This suggestion is confirmed by her reaction to the first of the dreams she reported. She accepted her father's attention to mother and stepmother as a kind of caretaking. The distancing from sexual content remained, though the degree to which she handled this content by denial or renunciation was not clear. Perhaps the fact that she was pregnant had reduced the intensity of the conflict. The cycles she experienced in the follow-up demonstrated that, as she expressed her feelings about the deaths in her family and dealt with the haunting images of the dead in a dyadic setting — reconstituting the security of the analytic alliance—her ego resources were enhanced for self-analytic work in the mastery of her conflicts.

Discussion

As the analytic process unfolds and the transference neurosis develops, the patient's recurrent patterns of conflict achieve a greater coherence and clarity. While there is no simple linearity or uniform sequence in the appearance of derivatives of conflict, certain regularities do emerge. The recurring pattern of conflicts we have demonstrated in this case is a convenient unit of observation for research purposes, and its study constitutes a powerful research tool deserving of further theoretical elaboration. Hendrick (1942) states that physiological maturation of the sensorimotor and intellectual apparatus involves repetitiveness, that this quality characterizes life, including all biological phenomena, and that it is implicit in the psychoanalytic concept of instincts as the source of recurrent tension and their gratification as tension release. As for psychopathology, Kubie (1941) describes repetitiveness as the essence of all neurotic manifestations, bearing the imprint of a biological process in "obligatory repetitions in which the distorted repetitive mechanism has for special reasons singled out now one and now another manifestation for repetitive emphasis" (p. 24). Kubie takes issue with Freud's explanation of blind and painful repetitiveness in terms of a repetition compulsion that draws its demonic power from masochism and the death instinct. Kubie views the neurotic process "as a pathological distortion of repetitive processes which, in and of themselves, are basically normal and ubiquitous in human psychology" (p. 38). But while there has been disagreement about the basis for repetitive phenomena, the fact that repetition occurs has never been in doubt.

In "Remembering, Repeating and Working Through," Freud (1914) wrote:

> We have learnt that the patient repeats instead of remembering, and repeats under the conditions of resistance. We may now ask what it is that he in fact repeats or acts out. The answer is that he repeats everything that has already made its way from the sources of the repressed into his manifest personality—his inhibitions and unserviceable attitudes and his pathological character-traits. He also repeats all his symptoms in the course of the treatment [p. 151].

Freud extended the compulsion to repeat to transference and resistance: "We soon perceive that the transference itself is only a piece of repetition, and that the repetition is a transference of the forgotten past not only on to the doctor but also on to all the other aspects of the current situation" (p. 151). In "Analysis Terminable and Interminable," Freud (1937) described the mechanisms of defense as "regular modes of reaction of [the patient's] character, which are repeated throughout his life whenever a situation occurs that is similar to the original one" (p. 237). This view of analysis corresponds to the consensus of a panel on separation-individuation in infancy (Winestein, 1973). There Settlage characterized human psychological development as a lifelong process of separation-individuation. The relationship between the psychoanalytic process and separation-individuation will be explored at length in subsequent chapters. Pfeffer (1963) notes that

> in analysis, repetition is not eliminated, but the content or substance of what is repeatable is changed. That is to say, the neurotic repeats the conflicts of the infantile past, whereas the satisfactorily analyzed patient in new situations that require mastery is capable, in addition, of repeating the *solutions* of the same conflicts as achieved in the analysis [p. 241].

We may readily anticipate a different view of repetitive cycles of conflict, namely, that they are the consequence of an inadequate or incomplete analysis. Such an outcome might be attributed to the severity of the patient's early traumatic experiences or the inexperience of the analyst. The analytic ideal of resolution of the Oedipus complex in the transference neuroses, which involves the obliteration of the complex and the redistribution of its elements in strong, reality-oriented psychic structures, would thereby be preserved. But to the extent that this ideal may constitute no more than an analytic myth, strict adherence to it may have unfortunate consequences. For it suggests that any analysis that does not have such an elegant result is a bad analysis, thereby creating a feeling of anxiety and narcissistic vulnerability for the analyst. Realistic achievements are not realistically valued. Psychoanalysis as a scientific enterprise suffers thereby, for the actual results of the analysis are not subjected to rigorous scrutiny in the literature, and the data accumulated in spontaneous follow-ups and re-analyses remain unpublished, incapable of raising pertinent questions and of expanding the base for a more sophisticated theory of therapy.

In "Analysis Terminable and Interminable," Freud (1937) raised the question as to whether conflicts can really be resolved. He emphasized that the taming of instinctual demands depends upon the strength of the instinct as opposed to the strength of the ego under a particular set of circumstances. He thus regarded quantitative issues as critical to the question of whether insecure repressions could be replaced by reliable ego-syntonic controls. He stressed that, while analysis did strengthen the forces of the ego, transformations were often only partial, and transitions and intermediate stages were more common than sharply differentiated opposite states. Moreover, the analyst's conviction as to the insights achieved was not necessarily fully shared by the patient. It was Freud's opinion that conflicts not spontaneously involved in the analytic process could not be artificially introduced by the analyst as a prophylactic measure, suggesting, therefore, that some conflicts inevitably remained unaddressed. Furthermore, his advice to the analyst that he renew his own analysis at five-year intervals clearly suggested his impression that conflicts were not necessarily permanently resolved and that exposure to new conflicts in work with patients was a professional hazard requiring attention. In the section dealing with resolution of conflict, Freud concluded that the available information at the time did not permit him to decide the question whether conflicts could theoretically be completely resolved. In our view, however, Freud's *approach* to the problem was of overriding significance. For he did not engage in speculation, dogmatic assertion, or polemic. He raised the question: "What is our experience?"

In that scientific tradition, then, what does our experience indicate? First, that there are repetitive patterns of conflict that bear the imprint of the developmental experience of the individual, including his analysis. The recurrence of conflict is speeded up by the experience of the analysis and the sensitization of the patient's ego to his internal processes. Second, that the significant outcome of the analysis is the development of a self-analytic function, as a complex coping mechanism. Environmental and internal stimulation in dynamic flux expose the individual to variations of the basic configuration of his conflict; optimally, the self-analytic function allows the patient to move in the direction of resolution. An analysis is thus an important developmental episode in the life of the individual; its termination is but a transitional phase in a continuing developmental history.

Follow-Up on the Follow-Up

In this case we have been able to follow some further developmental vicissitudes of the patient by means of a lengthy interview with her about her experiences in a second ongoing analysis. A second formal follow-up will have to await completion of her analytic experience. But the findings reported in this addendum bear out our conviction that second analyses constitute an untapped scientific resource in the study of the psychoanalytic process.

The patient returned to her analyst for further analysis when her daughter, with whom she was pregnant during the follow-up, was one-and-a-half years old. She was struggling with the need to wean her child and was not enthusiastic about sex. She felt like screaming when she was touched, a reaction reminiscent of past concerns in her analysis about being ripped open in sex. Her initial concerns were again about her analyst's competence, questioning whether he could understand, whether she might not need a woman analyst. She described a left-out feeling with young women of her acquaintance that was intensified by her role as a young mother. The mothering experience was clearly a central concern. In the first analysis, the analyst had attended to disruptive features in her relationship with women, including her conflict with her brother for her mother's attention, her penis envy, and her pseudomasculine toughness. The focus in the second analysis was on the underlying depression, how alone she felt, how left out. Her mother's busy activities in the community and conflicted identity as a woman had resulted in a considerable degree of early deprivation for the patient. After some recognition that these were the roots of her own conflict about giving up nursing and permitting her daughter some space for individuation, the patient pressed for termination. The analyst acknowledged her improvement but noted the need for further work on her depression. She felt hurt and depreciated, became brusque and cold, and revealed a sense of her defectiveness. The urge to terminate prematurely was motivated by anxiety and the need to prove herself whole and well. Her reaction was reminiscent of the exchange at termination of the first analysis in which, revealing her narcissistic vulnerability to the analyst's comment about the analysis being a pretty good one, she insisted that it had been excellent.

After something over a year of her second analysis, she became pregnant again, experienced a sense of injury at the analyst's absence in the summer vacation break, and spoke of her wish to present the baby to him as a gift. The theme of feeling hurt was present in her accounts of experiences with girlfriends and with her analyst. She readily felt depressed and depreciated. In the analytic work it was noted that she had projected onto her friends the role of internal critic that she had already assigned to her mother. She felt desperate, worthless, unappreciated, not in the center of interest of those she sought out. Her own brusque behavior as a disruptive factor in relationships was subjected to analytic scrutiny by focusing on subtle aspects of the interaction with her analyst. In her responses, she unwittingly maintained an invulnerable, arrogant posture, cutting off the analyst with a brief rejoinder and withdrawing. Such behavior had made it difficult to maintain her friendships with girlfriends particularly. The abrupt, even critical attitude she displayed was unmasked as a fear of her own neediness, an effort to avoid the friendly interest she desired so much.

The conflict was poignantly experienced in relation to her firstborn child, now four years old. The child had detached herself from the patient in reaction to her pregnancy, and become attached in turn to a neighbor whose motherliness was a friendly beacon. Her mother's self-absorption and difficulty picking her up and playing with her and later, her attention to the baby, were significant reasons for this temporary rupture. But a more important dynamic explanation became apparent. The patient had reacted to her daughter's frustration and disappointment, and her preference for the neighbor, by becoming hurt.

Then, fearing her own rage, she had withdrawn from her child into melancholy and helplessness except for occasional involuntary expressions of anger which had surprised her and reinforced the very behavior in her daughter that had prompted her misery.

She recognized such patterns of response in her analysis as well, in her reactions to arrangements for a change in appointment or a failure in empathy on the part of her analyst. The frustration and anger, and her characteristic response of brusqueness, coldness, and suppressed rage, were elaborated in memories of her interaction with her mother. Her mother had never felt good about herself and had dealt with her narcissistic vulnerabilities in a manner that served as a model for identification. Busy and preoccupied, the mother had never truly trusted her daughter and had maintained a constant expectation that she be a good girl and conceal any imperfection, that she subdue precocious inclinations and be slow, plodding, and dependable. A nagging quality had marked their interaction and commonly evoked shared feelings of lowered self esteem and depression. The patient herself had developed an early pseudo-independence. She would rise first, make her own breakfast, and turn to her father for attention. Her mother couldn't wait for her to grow up and stop being a burden, stop displaying the dependent needs that threatened her as well. In her relationship with her own daughter, then, the patient recognized that she had sought reassurance about herself and about her role as a mother in a variation on the theme of seeking reassurance as a child. She had expected her daughter to serve as a positive mirror. She had attempted to counteract the past by being more available and giving than her mother had been but had then experienced her daughter's independent strivings as a threat. The unravelling of the patient's conflicts over separation-individuation and the recognition of their expression in the transference and the relationship with her daughter and with her girl-friends now served to give her a perspective on the depression and allowed hostility to emerge in a less defended setting. The breach in relations with her daughter was healed and she grew more comfortable about accepting her own needs in the analytic situation.

The sexual relationship with her husband, however, continued to pose problems at this point in her analysis—when the follow-up on the follow-up occurred. Her interest was largely focused on the mother-child interaction. Moreover, her past experience of a masochistic type of sexual gratification had required some evidence of mistreatment for sexual pleasure and as a means of counteracting her guilt about incestuous wishes and biting impulses toward men. But her husband's kind and gentle behavior gave her little basis for feeling wounded; they liked the same things, enjoyed family outings, did things together a lot. Memories of her brother intruded on their relationship. Giving to him was like giving to her brother and was thus compromised by old jealousies. She reacted intensely to being touched in sexual activity. It made her feel overstimulated and irritable, arousing memories of past temper tantrums. She recalled an old boyfriend as an exciting sexual object, in contrast to her husband. The explanations adduced for her sexual difficulties in the first analysis had thus been insufficient and the need for further exploration was apparent to analyst and patient alike. Still, the central theme of her second analysis, at least to date, was clear. This was what the patient described as a third dimension in her comprehension of herself, an understanding of her melancholy in its characterological aspects, as it was based on her experience of separation-individuation.

We can see, then, that while the ingredients of the

pattern of conflict described some years earlier were again present in her account, the central focus of the second analytic effort had shifted from concerns about relating to men and marriage to problems with mothering, with greater attention to dyadic issues of tension regulation and early patterns of reaction. Her characterological armor, a brusque, disdainful attitude, was related to narcissistic issues surrounding fears of her own neediness and depression. Her problems with narcissism and tension regulation became even more apparent in her efforts to raise her daughter, reviving memories and mobilizing transferences that could be productively analyzed in their dyadic context. It is clear in this case, as in the case reported in the preceding chapter, that the developmental tasks of parenthood were a significant stimulus to the revival and analysis of early developmental issues in second analyses. Nevertheless, we regard our findings as also confirming one of the conclusions of our research, that such early determinants of symptoms and character are often not given sufficient attention in first analyses because of the analyst's view of the analytic task as centered on the resolution of neurotic oedipal conflicts.

Chapter 4

The Psychoanalytic Situation in a Development Context: The Fate of the Analytic Alliance

Analysts customarily hold that an analysis proceeds in a state of abstinence in which infantile wishes pressing for gratification in the transference neurosis are not, after all, gratified but analyzed. The real gratifications implicit in the "non-neurotic" transference, in the analytic alliance, have been less subject to analytic scrutiny, taken for granted as relatively silent elements in the ongoing process except as the process is interrupted by separations. Yet the effects of these gratifications are quite significant in the outcome, most dramatically in those instances in which the patient has had particular problems with the experience of separation-individuation early in life. Some may argue that the separation between the analytic alliance and the transference neurosis is an artificial one maintained entirely for heuristic purposes. If the regressive dyadic component of the oedipal configuration has been analyzed, would that not serve the mastery of separation and mourning in the termination phase? Would not the analysis of weekend separations, reactions to holidays and vacations as well as reactions to failures in analytic empathy provide sufficient material for an anticipatory working through of reactions to the loss of the "real" relationship at termination? In our follow-up work, this has not proven to be so. It seems necessary that we be even more attentive to the effects of the medium as we study the message.

CLINICAL ILLUSTRATIONS

We shall now review two case vignettes from our follow-up studies to illustrate the repetitive phenomena that first stimulated our interest in the post-analytic "intrapsychic metabolism" of the analytic alliance. We shall present as well an extended account of an analysis and its follow-up to elucidate the significance of the analytic alliance and its fate in the context of separation-individuation.

In the case cited in Chapter 2, the patient regularly sought out a friend who served as a sounding board, an external benign presence, when she was faced with heightened conflict. Verbalizing her thoughts and feelings in such a setting helped her to identify the problem and regain a sense of mastery. In her analytic experience, a defense transference of nagging dependence and excessive demands had been modified by the analyst's patient structuring behavior, with a benign maternal presence superimposed on the regressively conflicted and hostile mother imago. Although many features of her relationship with her mother had been analyzed, regressive demanding behavior and the analyst's structuring response had remained a prominent feature in the face of oedipal conflict at termination. Her alcoholic mother died shortly after termination of the analysis. She mourned her mother and her analyst simultaneously. As a result of the mourning for which she had been prepared by her analysis, she was enabled to secure a positive identification with her mother as an internalized resource that served to reduce the dread of oedipal conflict. The remarkable achievement of an oedipal solution and a successful marriage then took place post-analytically. The resolution was incomplete and yet happily effective. Her subsequent experience in a second analysis in exploring her problems with tension regulation has been reported in Chapter 2.

It is interesting to note that Norman (in Hurn, 1973) presented a follow-up experience in which the former analysand reported that in the face of increased stress, he summoned up the figure of his analyst as a "friendly spirit" in whose remembered presence the self-analytic task proceeded more expeditiously. In this instance, the internalized representation of the analyst served his accustomed role in an adaptive fantasy.

Our second case vignette concerns a 33-year-old teacher, the mother of two children, an attractive woman of medium height, responsive, quick, and articulate. Impulsivity and acquisitiveness were prominent features of her symptomatology strongly motivated by penis envy as well as a wish to make up for earlier feelings of deprivation. She was raised in a family disrupted by parental arguments and frequent moves. The defense transference was marked by an exaggerated display of helplessness which had strong regressive elements in it and an insistent desire for an object to comfort and rescue her. This behavior served as a way of handling stress in the face of heightened cathexis of oedipal conflict in her life. It operated as a kind of brinksmanship, effective because of her considerable charms in mobilizing psychotherapeutic responses, albeit confused by an admixture of seduction and anxiety that prompted an attenuation of contact.

The analysis focused on oedipal material. The analyst tended to regard the patient's dyadic problems as simply defensive, disregarding thereby a deficit in structure in the analytic alliance. The problem was one of emphasis and expectation. When the patient readily entered a transference neurosis of almost traumatic intensity, recapitulating the poorly structured experience of her childhood, the analyst did not address himself to the issue of tension regulation but was intent on interpreting the oedipal conflicts. In the family setting the pressure was toward compliance and some degree of premature adaptive mastery. The task of structuring and securing the development of a self-soothing function through attention to this aspect of the patient's anxiety was not pursued. Instead, the matrix of the analytic situation was formed of an amalgam of compliance on the part of the patient and kindly goal-directed effort on the part of the analyst. It permitted the unfolding of oedipal conflicts and some effective analytic work that benefited from the analyst's comprehension and interpretations but did not fully involve or promote the patient's self-analytic function. It was a successful analysis in many of its results. Its limitations seemed to be attributable to defects in the analytic alliance; namely, at follow-up the patient showed an excessive reliance on friends and husband to control her impulsivity and to provide a benign external facilitation of her problem-solving activities, in addition to excessive compliance and premature mastery. Problems with aggression in a dyadic context seemed related to a fascination with mourning and indicative of an inadequate mastery of separation-individuation conflicts.

The following extended case report elaborates the issues involved in the fate of the analytic alliance at significant points in the process and at follow-up.

CASE 3

The patient was a 30-year-old unmarried psychologist, well-groomed, attractive, quite reserved and youthful in appearance. Her presenting complaint was a problem in relating to men. She was interested in men who were distant and noncommital and tended to withdraw when a man showed interest. She had suffered the breaking up of an affair some six months earlier, an experience which had precipitated her seeking analysis. The affair had involved a mutually satisfying sexual relationship for a year but had been rudely interrupted when her boyfriend "discovered in a conversation" the superficiality of their relationship, that they both felt unable to commit themselves to anything deeper or more permanent. She recognized a repetitive pattern of such experiences in her life and sought help with it.

She was the only child in a family in which secrecy was prized and communication difficult. Her mother's life had been marred by her own illegitimate birth and a brief unsuccessful marriage prior to her marriage to the patient's father. These facts were seriously stigmatizing in the community in which the patient had been raised. As an example of the problem in communication, the patient recalled that at the age of six she had run into the house from her play to ask her mother if she had been married before. Her mother said "yes" and she ran out again. The next time she raised the question she was in college.

At the patient's birth, the mother suffered a serious depression and the patient was cared for by her grandparents. Her father took on some of the maternal role as well. Mother was hypochondriacal and phobic, preoccupied with bowel functions. Her approach to childrearing was behavioristic and repressive. Mother's ailments were a source of family concern. Her father attempted to be supportive of his wife's needs and would caution the patient not to disturb her mother. He conveyed to her the idea that she had done enough harm by being born. The patient shared a room with her parents, sleeping with her mother because her parents did not sleep together. She experienced a kind of intimacy with her mother in thus displacing her father. She was also treated as a confidante by her father who talked to her about his sexual problems with her mother, for whom sex was dirty and objectionable. These "special" relationships with her parents were ostensibly gratifying but fraught with anxiety and superficial in nature. There were more positive features in her childhood experiences with her grandparents as parental substitutes and she grew up with a capacity to relate to girlfriends as supportive figures in spite of the very obvious problems with her mother.

Initial Assessment

The highlights of our assessment of the first few hours of the analysis may serve as a baseline for discussion of this case. The defense transference presented itself in the form of a "good girl" compliance and a characteristic tendency toward both attracting and pushing away those who interested her, thereby maintaining an ungratifying superficiality in her relationships. There were immediate problems about communication with a tendency toward fragmentary and disjointed accounts of her experiences. A nascent transference thread ran through the material involving difficulties in talking to her parents. Her initial presentation suggested immaturity, passivity, and a search for structure. Historically, she described a recurrent need to go home to her parents when she suffered disappointment or serious stress, indicating that they somehow constituted a supportive resource in spite of all the conflict with them. She described relationships with women friends as reassuring and their support as effective in helping her overcome her initial anxiety in the analysis. Going to girlfriends on weekends for support was an adaptive measure reminiscent of her being farmed out to relatives as a child. It served to interrupt any threatened fragmentation of her self and correct for any sense of deprivation.

The use of the couch was stressful to her because of the loss of eye contact and the analyst's silence. In the first couch hour a fearful fantasy of a sick bedridden patient was mobilized in conjunction with memories of her mother as a phobic woman for whom enemas were a common remedy for hypochondriacal concerns about her bowels. She described her mother as controlling her with illnesses and fears. With the patient's acceptance as an analytic patient, she experienced a crescendo of charged emotion, almost like an enema response. There was evidence of an identification with her mother, full of anxiety and easily disrupted, with distancing as a solution. She described anaclitic qualities in her relationship with her mother, an overprotective containment of her problems.

Her first dreams followed a weekend interruption and the first use of the couch. In the first, she was coming to the office for a regularly scheduled appointment and the waiting room was full of people. She came in and started to talk but discovered it was not her analyst behind the couch. A receptionist explained that she was there for tests that her analyst had ordered—prints of elbows and feet. She responded sarcastically, "It's like phrenology, only elbows and feet instead of bumps on the head." In the second, four girls wanted to room with her but she discovered it would be cheaper to be by herself, so she didn't room with them.

Her sense of deprivation is suggested in the expression of anger and sarcasm in the dream. The complaints about the secretary may have referred to the analyst's notetaking, expressing a wish for special attention. The woman intruding between her and the man introduced a repetitive dream theme. The intrusion expressed simultaneously a regressive desire for maternal nurture and an impatiently perceived distancing defense in relating to a man. The reference to four friends alluded to the four analytic hours per week. The decision not to room with her girlfriends suggested a positive commitment to confronting her problems with men. Her association was to her interest in a big man on campus in college.

The dreams suggested a conflict-ridden cathexis of an oedipal theme with regressive features that stressed dyadic problems. Her recall of a childhood experience tended to confirm this formulation. She remembered her fearful distortion of a picture belonging to her grandfather. It seemed to her as a child that it was a picture of a lady with a feather in her hat—who appeared to be in mourning, all dressed in black. Her grandfather took it to his office. When she saw the picture again in high school, it was of three horses running. Her grandfather reminded her of her early childhood fears of the picture and when she tried, she could rediscover the outlines of the old distorted picture. Her grandmother had used her misperception of the picture to frighten her into being good, threatening to show her the picture of the "meanie" if she misbehaved. Her regressive fantasy transformed a scene with phallic qualities into a nightmarish witch-like figure.

In spite of her caution and phobic reaction to the uneasy cathexis of oedipal material, she was able to describe her problems and their patterned nature in a self-observing fashion, and to experience and report her feelings. Her introspective capacity was quickly evident in the quality of her reports of behavior with friends and family and in the analytic situation, and included much significant information (experiential details, memories, and fantasies) as evidence of a preconscious synthetic function. Regressive reactions were excessive with problems in tension regulation, complaints of upsetting feelings and of "things going too fast." However, she was able to tolerate her anxiety by expressing it and appealing for help. Weekend separations were readily manageable. She expressed her determination to work with her reactions and not retreat into wishes to be rescued. Her penchant for compliance appeared to be a threat to her genuine participation in the analysis and the development of a self-analytic function. In fact, she reported experiencing an authentic and false self in her development. As a youngster, she had a nickname for her true self. The false self was a pretense at maturity and self-sufficiency, an adaptive solution related genetically to her mother's expectations and "behavioral treatment." Her ability to recognize and report such phenomena and her determination to be herself were hopeful notes at the onset of the process.

Course of the Analysis

Early in the analysis the patient experienced intense affects, especially around separations, and a marked narcissistic vulnerability. These affective states would lead to sudden experiences of numbness in general or in a specific body part. At other times and later in the analysis, she suffered severe headaches or illness. These somatization reactions became intelligible as a discharge channel for her rage. She reported and worked through dreams of her mother's death, learning to tolerate her anger as a psychological experience. She became aware that her own inhibitions and bodily concerns were an identification or merger with her phobic mother as a shield against her anger and an effort to preserve the relationship. As she elaborated memories associated with her tears, she overcame her fear of crying on the couch. She reported that, according to her mother's boasts, she had been taught at nine months not to put things in her mouth and was completely toilet trained by 18 months. By the age of two, she could be taken anywhere with complete confidence that she would not touch anything. She painfully concluded that she had suffered an exaggerated suppression of her feelings and activities as a child and was bitter about her mother's pride in a pathological state of affairs.

As the analysis proceeded she experienced fears of her own omnipotence in the form of a concern that she might induce her analyst to feel what she felt. She remembered that as a child she would cause her mother to feel ill by any accusation or expression of rage and that her father would take her away to calm the situation. Her guilt about her mother's illnesses was explored and related genetically to childhood anality and the struggle about enemas and bowel control. The intrusive woman of her dreams was clearly identified in this context as a figure disrupting her efforts to relate to men.

Her dreams began to shift to an interest in men. She reported recollections about her father and expressed curiosity about her analyst's family. In the second year of her analysis, she reported a dream in which the analyst's wife entered the consulting room during the hour. She expected that her analyst would make his wife leave but the analyst did nothing. She felt angry and helpless. The analyst's wife represented her view of her mother as a childhood witch and the analyst's passivity her father's inability to respond in a consistently protective manner. In her associations she recalled that when her mother took enemas she would enter the living room where the patient and her father sat talking. Her mother would giggle and announce in a childlike voice that she was full of water. She would then dance around the floor and her father would laugh as though he were a spectator at a show. In describing these scenes, the patient sadly realized that she felt competitive with her mother for attention and the right to be a child. In many ways she had been placed in the position of being a mother to her mother.

As these memories were revived and their significance worked through, several changes were noted. The patient lost her fey quality and became pretty, feminine, and alive. She found sustenance in the memory of her paternal grandparents whom she had dearly loved. The analyst became more real to her and remained a real object during separations. Her anger about separations became more tolerable to her. She had dreams and associations expressing her sexual feelings toward her analyst and was pleased that she could feel warmth and sexuality simultaneously toward a man. In her feelings about her father in the past she had been overwhelmed with fears of her omnipotence and feelings of guilt. Her general improvement was accompanied by tears for the unhappy child she had been and a recognition of the need to separate and mourn the loss of her analyst in the termination of the analysis.

Termination

At the time of discussion about the possibility of termination the patient characteristically reacted to the stress with a decision to go home and visit her parents. She had been concerned about her relationship with a current boyfriend who was more in touch with her and yet unsuitable for marriage. She displaced some of her feelings in the analysis onto her boyfriend, struggling with the idea of an impending loss of a relationship without losing herself. The thought of saying good-by was mind-boggling to her. She expressed gratitude for what she had gained and tears for what she would lose. A regressive trend followed with concerns about disappointment and abandonment in her relationship with her boyfriend. She half humorously anticipated a weeklong migraine headache on her visit home. Her reactions brought into focus a continued vulnerability in object constancy, tension regulation, and her capacity for self-soothing, requiring external confirmation of her worth as an individual in the face of the threat of separation.

She left with a feeling of hurt and disappointment about her boyfriend's casual response to her trip. On her return her feelings went unresolved with her boyfriend (and in the transference) because she avoided them. She described the nature of her experience with men in terms of situations that had been imposed on her. In an apparent identification with her mother she cited her mother's recall of her father's terms for dating, which were simply that everything proceed in accordance with his wishes. Women did not ask for what they wanted. When the analyst asked if she had thought of a time to terminate, she told him she preferred that he set the date.

The patient revealed the facts she had gleaned from the exercise of her curiosity in conversation with her mother at home, crying for herself as a child. Her mother had had migraine headaches throughout her pregnancy and for the first nine months of the patient's life was constantly ill. She could not eat or sleep and her weight fell to 90 pounds. The patient and her mother were both cared for by the maternal grandmother. Mother took to her bed and both were a burden. As a child she was passed around among relatives, though not because she was wanted. As she reviewed these unhappy details, she asked the analyst, "Why haven't I felt like a burden to you?" She expressed her feeling that the analysis had been a positive experience and sought some information from the analyst that his expectations had been met. He obliged with an honest regard for their accomplishment. In an unconscious response to the patient's apparent need for direct reassurance, he sat in the wrong chair when the patient entered the consulting room, as though for a psychotherapeutic sitting-up session. The patient was amused and recognized that the termination was new for him too in the conduct of an analytic process. In this context, she asked the analyst to set a date for termination. While the analyst responded to the patient's defensive superficial need to be told what to do, he failed to recognize and pursue the analytic task—to explore the derivatives of early childhood experience that constituted impediments to a development of independent tension regulatory functions. He complied, setting a date five months in advance and thereby providing the patient with an "imposed solution." The depths that were plumbed in this period can be illustrated by an insight of the patient some two weeks later. She had complained about a lack of warmth and feelings of exclusion at work to a sympathetic colleague. She recalled that as a child her crib had been placed in the hallway and that she had kept a close watch on everyone. Such monitoring activity had continued all her life and she had attributed it to her sensitivity and caring but she now noted that it was a security operation motivated by concerns for herself.

In describing her status she posed the fact that she

had not resolved her problem with men. Her analyst interpreted her disappointment that she would be ending her analysis without involvement with a man as an oedipal disillusionment. Her response was that her parents were aware of their limitations and helped her get away. She recalled tearfully that her grandfather had held her, not her mother, and that if she had ever had cause to scream, her father raised his fist. She marvelled that she had grown up with any self-esteem at all. Her interest in a man was compromised by her fears of humiliation and abandonment as dyadic problems were engaged. She experienced old feelings of fatness, self-consciousness, and unlovability, attributed them to the prospect of termination, and reassured herself with thoughts that another man would come along and that she really did like herself better—a "good girl" solution.

As she complained of extra-analytic problems, her analyst more actively interpreted the evidence of denial of her disappointment in the analysis. The patient said that she was not in touch with such feelings in the transference and insisted that she felt very good and optimistic. She stated flatly that she did not want more analysis but a friend. What she sought were mirroring responses and the kind of mothering that might have permitted a more optimal individuation. The oedipal conflict was reproduced in a dream: "A man was attracting me and looking at another girl. I had had it and I left." The oedipal interpretation was stated in their shared metaphor as the analyst said, "It was the theme of the other woman again." The patient confirmed it with the thought that if the man were not married, he would choose her. She recognized the thought as a familiar friend that saved her sadness and loneliness. It was followed by headaches, feeling ill, and struggling against crying because she seemed an ugly sight when she looked in the mirror. Her response

to oedipal conflict and to termination was the mobilization of earlier problems in separation-individuation that
threatened the consolidation of her ego resources and her
self-concept. She described the essence of the problem in
a revealing anecdote. Someone asked her a question: "If
you went to a party and were not dressed right, would
you be upset?" In response to the question she recalled
an incident in adolescence. She was in junior high and
her mother had bought her a pair of loafers. They were
orange. She was always insecure and depended on her
mother to tell her what to wear. A mean teacher joked
about her orange loafers in a cruel and insensitive manner. She reported it to her mother who said, "Those are
spring shoes, you should not have worn them." Her
mother's need for approval was so great that she added,
"I hope nobody thinks I told you to wear them." The narcissistic burden was clear in the lack of support for her
tentative steps toward independent functioning. She
never wore the shoes again. Her analyst noted that she
had been abandoned by her mother in her distress and
that she feared a similar reaction from the analyst. The
patient angrily described her impulse to cry as a kind of
defeat, as though crying were for the analyst's gratification, like crying for her mother.

What the patient was experiencing so poignantly at
this point might be viewed as a version of her rapprochement crisis. Interpretation of the dyadic material as a
defense had maintained the emphasis on the dynamics
of oedipal conflict as crucial, whereas for this patient the
dyadic problem was critical in its own right and deserving
of an analytic effort to work through earlier issues of
separation-individuation. The approach to saying good-
by was "mind-boggling" because it was not conceived as
a step-by-step process attuned to the patient's capacity
for tension regulation and her ability to solve conflicts.

The analyst maintained a generally sympathetic posture more consistent with a psychotherapeutic effort than an analytic approach to the issues involved. Exposure of the patient's fears about her independent strivings, reproduced in a transference context without an "imposed solution" in setting the date, might have permitted a careful resolution of her painful early encounters with her mother with transmuting internalizations to lend stability to her capacity for self-soothing and tension regulation and thereby to permit a genuine consolidation of her resources in the solution of oedipal conflict.

Her final dreams provided a view of her frame of mind at termination. She reported the first on Thursday: "I was in a department store in a restroom. This woman was trying to get into the compartment I was in. But I won. I got rid of her." The second on Friday: "The elevator operator at the hospital. He makes passes at me. I get some gratification. But in the dream he gets more aggressive. I realized it was not possible." The patient regarded the dreams as a summary of her reactions. She identified the woman as mother because the bathroom was her room. In a telling comment about the action in the dream, she said that it was easier to get rid of the woman than to let her stay. She related it to being able to cry. This uneasy solution to her problems with her mother set the stage for continued lack of fulfillment in her relationship with a man. As a further association she reported another brief dream: "I said maybe I should go into therapy once a week. You said 'It's a good idea.' " In association she hinted at an adaptive solution seeking out as friends people who had had analysis, with the implicit message that they might serve as substitutes for the therapeutic environment. In talking about how unnatural termination felt, she registered her distress. But she also emphasized a feeling of excitement and a burst of energy and expressed pride in having overcome her old habit of obsessing. She was pleased that she had been able to avoid her headaches and face her sadness about leaving. She cried about how she would miss her analyst but moved with determination to the end of the process on the scheduled date. In the final session, she expressed gratitude, excitement, apprehension, and tears. It was evidence of a general improvement, but in the context of compliance.

Follow-Up Study

Six follow-up interviews were scheduled at weekly intervals 18 months after termination with the patient's ready agreement to participate in the research. The defense transference was immediately evident in her emphasis on how good an analysis she had experienced. She described the timing, termination, and changes as positive, adding that while some people might be angry at their analyst at termination, this was certainly not the case with her. She then acknowledged that the months following termination had been characterized by a quiet withdrawal. Some eight months after her analysis she had received word of the availability of a larger apartment for which she had applied. With the decision to move she had had an intense emotional response which she recognized as a delayed reaction to the end of her analysis. It was as though the apartment in which she lived was where she had grown up and the move was like leaving home. The pain was more intense than anything she had felt in her analysis. She had experienced a regression that required a couple of months of effort to overcome. She had thought of a return visit to her analyst but decided she could manage it herself.

On the first anniversary of her termination, her

professional life had blossomed with a promotion and rewarding work. She decided to do something about her
social life. In a sense her decision was a response to the
letter about the follow-up research. She wanted to demonstrate the effectiveness of her analysis in the area for
which she had sought help, namely, her relationships
with men. She met a man who was different from previous
boyfriends in that he was really interested in her. She
could communicate, feel some dependency, reveal herself
to him, and let him respond to her. Having thus cited her
improvement, she described some disappointment with
friends early in her analysis who had not been able to
accept her increased tolerance of her own needs. In conjunction with this disappointment, she expressed anger
at her parents for "closet issues," areas of deception which
she could not explore in a forthright fashion because her
mother could not be troubled and her father was lacking
in empathy. Her own complaints brought about a breach
in her defenses in the first session and she responded
with the thought that she regarded the follow-up as an
opportunity for us to "staff" her.

In the second interview, she revealed that she had
suffered lower abdominal and back pain for the past
month together with a low-grade fever. Her gynecologist
had diagnosed a viral disease and put her on pain med-
ication and an antibiotic. She promptly had a drug reaction. She was then informed on a subsequent visit that
she might need a hysterectomy and this caused her to
seek consultation from an internist and a second gynecologist. She had not mentioned her symptoms in the first
interview with the follow-up analyst because she feared
he would regard them as a complication and discontinue
the follow-up. In response to a question about whether
she had had any reactions to the first session, she reported
she had had a bad dream the night before but had at-

tributed it to receiving a Valentine's Day card from her mother. The card had contained an explicit warning that she might be hurt if she got too involved with her boyfriend and he then broke off the relationship. The message was blatant and strange. Her mother's injunctions about closeness with men had been incorporated by precept and example in a form that did not usually require verbal reinforcement. Perhaps it was evidence of her mother's awareness of the change in her approach to a man, her willingness to put more at risk. After receiving the card, she called her girlfriend to discuss it and even began to regard it as funny once she expressed an initial reaction of fury. She thought she had her reactions under control. Then came the dream.

In the dream her boyfriend had gone someplace in a convertible with two women. He stopped somewhere and was flirtatious with a woman right in front of her. She confronted him vigorously. She developed a severe headache while dreaming. When she awoke and realized it was a dream, she felt a sense of relief and the headache receded. She continued to feel bad physically, headachy and with some stomach distress. She recalled that she had suffered from headaches for some 10 to 15 years and that they had subsided during her analysis and that she had not had them recently. The dream was like a return to the past triggered by her mother's card (and the follow-up session).

In her effort to understand the dream, she noted that the two women were a recurring theme of her analysis. She had always monitored her feelings with regard to other women. She recalled the picture from her childhood (age three-four), the scene of three horses which she had transformed into a picture of an ugly woman with a pointed face and a black hat out of which protruded a big black feather. The woman was dressed in black and

looked mean and stern. In retrospect, it was like a Ror-
schach. The card reawakened her feelings that women
were not to be trusted. Her response in the dream was
to the woman as a competitor. She was impressed with
the fact that she didn't take it passively. She yelled out
and confronted her boyfriend.

She recalled that in her analysis she had talked about
men as though they were subjects for experimentation.
With her current boyfriend as well, she felt that she was
trying things out. She said that she had a lot more comfort
now with spontaneity. Her boyfriend didn't engage in
pretensions, and said what he thought. In the past, in
any relationship with a man she had always felt that she
had to try to please him. Now she tried to be herself and
it scared her. This was particularly true in expressing
anger. She worried about disagreements, but she did not
let them rest. She returned to them even if belatedly and
risked clarification.

The follow-up analyst asked if there were any sexual
problems with her boyfriend. After momentary suspicion
and a searching look, she proceeded to talk openly. She
did have concerns about venereal disease as a cause of
her symptoms, as did her gynecologist. The culture was
negative. Her boyfriend reacted very reasonably to her
apprehensions. He went to his own physician for a check
up that also proved negative. He accepted her gynecologist's recommendation against any sexual activity while
the basis for her physical distress remained in doubt.

She had experienced the onset of her physical symptoms as a disruption just when everything was going so
right. Her new apartment was comfortable, her promotion at work meaningful, and she had met a man she
liked. She struggled with a cynical reaction that things
were not supposed to go right for her. It was ironic. She
elaborated her efforts to pursue objective medical opin-

ions about her physical condition and yet to stay in touch with her psychological reactions as well. She knew that closeness was a problem for her. Things had changed a great deal but it was still a vulnerable area. When the follow-up analyst acknowledged her grasp of the situation, she said that part of the reason she wanted to continue these sessions was the opportunity they afforded to look within herself.

In the third session, she reported feeling better physically. Medical opinions about her gynecological problem had been reassuring. She felt as though she had been on a merry-go-round since her decision to move. She needed a chance to stop and have some space for maneuver. In fact, she recalled that she had the thought some weeks earlier that perhaps she would get sick. It was like a premonition that things were moving out of her control. She described a split in her behavior. At work she was a "head" person, but in her social interactions she turned off her thoughts. The follow-up analyst suggested the possibility that to know and explore her relations with men might seem off limits, like the "closet issues" with her parents. She felt criticized by the comment, emphasizing that she wanted to just experience things with her boyfriend and not question them. When asked about her feeling pressured as though she were on a merry-go-round, she described a sense of vulnerability because intense feelings of excitement, curiosity, and pleasure had been taboo at home.

In the fourth session she reported that her physical improvement had been sustained. Her manner was hesitant. She noted that once a week was different from four times a week, that she had somehow found herself talking in a free association style to her friends. Her boyfriend was leaving for a weekend to visit some friends. She had experienced the prospect of an interruption in their re-

lationship with a sense of relief and found herself preoccupied with thoughts of how to do a successful termination.
Her position in the chair with arms over her head seemed
more appropriate for lying on the couch. Her further associations led to the termination of her analysis with a
focus on her concern then about what it was appropriate
to experience and feel. The follow-up analyst suggested
that her anxiety had interfered with her acknowledgment
of what she did feel. She protested that while in the past
she had a need to appear strong and adequate, she now
allowed herself dependency. She had friends and health-
ier relationships and she experienced feelings appropriate to the situation, feelings she was supposed to have.
Again the emphasis on what she was supposed to feel was
brought to her attention. She acknowledged the repetition and recalled again that there was no rockiness or
storminess at the termination of her analysis.

In response to a suggestion that she was experiencing
feelings in the follow-up session similar to what she had
felt at the termination of her analysis, she said that it
was really hard for her to know. She had grown up in an
environment of do's and don'ts and should's and shouldn'ts,
but she just didn't know. She had returned to her analyst's building and been surprised that she could not recall what floor his office was on. Her thoughts had led to
anger on her job, confrontations with a director, and fantasies about leaving without decent references. She
thought of her analyst as a good reference. The concern
about the anger implicit in her comments was highlighted. She denied any awareness of anger about termination. After some hesitation she brightened and
thought of her recent description of the struggle about
expressing anger with her boyfriend. With a grin, she
reported that in her experience she tended to think that
"they" were angry and then the feeling came crashing

through that the anger was her own. She reiterated that it was hard to be aware of what she felt about termination. The follow-up analyst commented that perhaps it would be possible to see what her reactions were in the follow-up. Her response was to question how many sessions were left as though she had lost count. On leaving the session, she mentioned that she would probably be out of town to visit her parents for a week, the week after next, and wondered if we could reschedule her last appointment. She then cancelled her next appointment during the week because she was too busy with preparations for leaving.

The visit to her parents punctuated her concerns about termination, repeating her experience in the termination phase of her analysis, and once again suggesting a characteristic response to stress. She returned with the complaint that she felt drained by all her activities as though she had not been on vacation. She complained of her insecurity with her boyfriend, noting how much she was inclined to project. With any approach to intimacy she needed reassurance. Her strange sense of timing led to inappropriate confrontations. She would voice her questions two days after a conversation in which a misunderstanding had occurred. Then it would be hard to recapture the context and to know what had been her and what him. She easily felt lonely and rejected, and couldn't sustain any constancy. She had explained all this to her boyfriend. While she was away, he had called her and she had felt good and close to him but again the continuity was hard to maintain. The follow-up analyst attempted to relate her concerns about rejection and continuity to the interruption in the follow-up sessions but these efforts were met with denial. She was aware of her problems with her boyfriend. She knew that she ran hot and cold. It was easier to see her ambivalence out there.

She said that she preferred just to experience things and not examine them even if it meant flubbing around and seeing what happened. She could tolerate it. It was scary for her to expose her needs and feelings and not be fully in command but she was doing it. She experienced wild fears of rejection but she voiced them. When her boyfriend called in a cheery fashion she was relieved. He had heard her and understood. She needed relationships to counteract her fears. In the past, there were failures in relationships around her experience of anger. She would read what people wanted and be that, losing herself in the process. Now she fought it out even if it was frightening.

In the termination of her analysis she had not thought about anger. What was paramount for her was the corrective experience with her analyst. She had been able to relate to a man who was not like her father. It was so exciting. She could not connect anger with the end of her analysis. At termination there had still been a stable world and there had been growing pains. She had cut off a relationship with a guy who had disappointed her with his lack of empathy (thereby displacing her anger toward the analyst onto him).

She emphasized that her fearfulness about the responses of others made her expressions of anger awkward but that her feelings were insistent and that she was willing to give them expression. With some help from the follow-up analyst, she acknowledged that she regarded the follow-up sessions as demanding and felt them to be an intrusion. Her cancellation had been prompted by "a feeling that she was up to here with the sessions." She questioned the timing of the follow-up because so much was going on in her life, yet noted the contradiction in her feelings in that she had wanted the opportunity to review her analysis at the beginning. She complained that it was hard work to dissect everything. She did not want an analytic effort now. She felt that she had the tools herself and close friends to serve as a kind of support system when she needed them. As the session ended she asked, "Do you want me to come in next week?" The follow-up analyst asked her what she wanted to do. She said she expected six sessions as arranged and would like to come in and finish up.

In the final interview she indicated an interest in any research paper that might result from her experience. She denied any concern about how she was viewed. On the one hand she emphasized her awareness that the follow-up was not analysis; on the other, she remarked how strange it was because the analytic process was part of the research. She had not expected that and didn't like the intrusion. She added ambivalently that she had anticipated talking more about the present and yet she hadn't. After a long silence with eyes downcast and a depressive note, she responded to a question about her thoughts with the comment that there was nothing on her mind. With a smile she added that there probably would be next week. She emphasized that she does have good friends who help her when she hits a snag. They are not therapists, but friends. They talk things out with each other. As a result of her analysis she has chosen friends with whom that is possible and she is free to express how she really feels. She has been insisting on talking things out with her boyfriend too. She and her friends are acutely aware of her exaggerated need for control. It's a joke between them that they have a celebration when she blows it and displays her dependency and vulnerability. There is no hostility or mockery in that. They are necessary for her.

She recalled part of a dream the night before last of a conflict with her boyfriend. It was strange because actually they had had a good time the night before. Conflict and the threat of repetition were always with her. Was he mad at her or was she mad at him? It was easy to get confused. She might act in a rejecting way when she feared rejection. As the session drew to a close she re-iterated her feeling that her analysis had been really good. She emphasized her freedom of expression and her continuing effort to represent herself genuinely. She stated it somewhat defensively, with a sidelong glance at the follow-up analyst, who confirmed her self-obser-vation and thanked her for her participation in the proj-ect.

Resume of the Follow-Up

The course of the follow-up involved an initial defense transference, a renewal of interest in her conflicts, and a clear restatement of oedipal conflict in the dream, with dyadic elements recathected in the concerns about her mother's Valentine's Day warning. The dyadic context remained problematic, interfering with the resolution of the oedipal conflict. However, the patient was actively engaged in confronting her problems. The figure of her "good analyst" was an important resource to which she turned in fantasy, "a reference point" protected from crit-icism by displacement of her anger. As a benign internal presence he helped counteract the disruptive effect of the hostile currents projected and denied, and which then came crashing through as her own feelings. The friends she found served to support the benign outcomes of her stormy misunderstandings. In this ambience, she was in-creasingly able to risk free expression of her feelings with a man. She created a psychotherapeutic setting for her dyadic problems and was not interested in their analysis. Her visits home remained a response to stress with the ameliorated features she had noted after her trip home in the termination phase of the analysis. The changes were maintained. She did not experience migraine headaches and she was able in her contacts with them to explore details of her early history in a manner that was quite impossible prior to her analysis. The continued struggle evident in her behavior seemed to be indicative of an ongoing process with a promise of further progressive change.

The fate of the alliance was evident in the patient's post-analytic experience. She demonstrated acquired skills in self-observation, the analysis of dreams and behavior, and a continued quest for self-realization. Her analyst remained a benign presence, his influence apparent in her informed selection of supportive friends. In the follow-up, her vulnerability in a dyadic context became apparent when she was confronted with her emphasis on having the "right" feelings and reactions at termination. The theme of the orange loafers hovered in the background, shielded from analytic review by her defensive reaction. She was clearly better able to risk the expression of her feelings but with limitations and conditions. There was a threat to object constancy in her denial and projective defenses and she relied on her friends to absorb the impact of her behavior when she was not self-aware and able to integrate it. Her preference for growth by experience, free of self-consciousness and obsessive thought, was developmentally promising but limited the current acquisition of insight. There was a tendency to take flight when the intensity of her affects mounted. Independent action, whether in the form of self-expression or the resolution of oedipal conflict, was compromised by her need to return to her narcissistically vulnerable mother and reestablish a sense of security based on her continued presence and approval. Illness remained a means of tension control based on an identification with her hypochondriacal mother, bringing about a kind of reunion with her.

In this case, the analytic alliance was compromised by a transference-countertransference interaction at termination. The patient's wishes for reassurance and an imposed solution evoked active responses in the analyst. He was moved unconsciously to convert the analytic situation into a psychotherapeutic setting by taking his seat for a face-to-face encounter instead of behind the couch on one occasion. He acted in a kindly gratifying manner in acknowledging his actions had the effect of supporting the patient's wish to preserve the image of her analyst as a good mother and to subdue the turmoil about separation, leaving the patient unaware of the nature of her anger and her conflicts about separation-individuation. In a modified form, the solution at termination repeated the familiar pattern with her mother and the presence of kindly analytic surrogates postanalytically was a necessary ingredient in her adaptation.

The follow-up study obviously could not afford an appropriate context for an analytic investigation of these derivatives of her rapprochement crisis. Her rejection of such an effort seemed quite realistic. We do feel warranted, however, in stressing the potential usefulness of an analytic approach to the issue of separation-individuation as it is engaged in the analytic alliance, rather than a simple reliance on the psychotherapeutic effects of that alliance.

Chapter 6

A Clinical Study of the Defense Transference

In the following case presentation, we focus on the defense transference—its emergence, repetition, and management—in the analysis and in the follow-up. Our purpose is to demonstrate its function as a coping mechanism and as a defense, and to elaborate our hypothesis that its roots are in the experience of separation-individuation, constituting a solution to object relational conflicts. We shall spell out the implications of such a view in the final chapter.

CASE 4

The patient was a 28-year-old single Jewish musician. Her chief complaint was an inability to commit herself to enduring and gratifying relationships with men, although she became involved in intense encounters. She related this to the death of her father and a brother five years her senior in an automobile accident when she was nine years old. She experienced men as fatherly or brotherly, and sexual relations were problematic, with frigidity prominent. She had a close friendship with a married man 20 years her senior, platonic in nature, and readily characterized as a father-daughter relationship. Some two years prior to her analysis, in connection with a brief affair, she had become pregnant and had had an abortion. Her despondency and her view of the abortion as a way to commit suicide had alarmed her and prompted a nine-month psychotherapy on a once-a-week basis. She had found it helpful, in spite of her feeling that the psychiatrist was outmoded and moralistic. She had recognized her need for analysis and applied to the Institute Clinic.

Born and raised in a large metropolis in the Northeast, her description of her early life centered on the traumatic loss of her father and brother. Memories of her father, a successful accountant, were sparse. She remembered only his "masculine traits"—his shirts, ties, etc. Her mother was described as a short, heavy woman, quite self-sufficient. She recalled that, as a young girl, everything had revolved around her brother, who had been the most important person in her life. She regarded him as favored by both parents. When she was eight years old, her family had worried about her tomboyish behavior. She had refused to wear dresses and had tried to imitate her brother in many ways.

At the time of the accident, the family had been vacationing with her maternal grandfather. She recalled her anger that she had not been allowed to accompany her brother and father on their fatal excursion, and that she felt responsible for their deaths and guilty toward her mother. She had been informed of the accident by her mother, who had advised her to pray. She had maintained a persistent fantasy that her father and brother were still alive, and would recurrently look up their names in telephone directories, as though to discover their current abode. Within a few months of the accident, the patient had been dispatched to a summer camp while her mother accompanied the maternal grandfather on a trip to Europe. On their reunion in the fall, they had moved to a smaller house, and for six months the patient had suffered a serious depression, refusing to go to school or to let her mother out of her sight. This reaction had subsided slowly. She had been seen by a psychiatrist, who had minimized her psychopathology, after which she had been able to return to school, without any further psychotherapeutic experience in childhood.

Opening Phase of Analysis

In the early sessions of the analysis, in conjunction with the presentation of significant historical and current material, a characteristic pattern emerged in her relationship with the analyst. She challenged his professional status and questioned the distinction between analysis and therapy and his knowledge of her intake interviews at the Clinic. The challenge had a teasing quality as well. She persistently pursued the issue of whether he was Jewish, expressing her need for understanding from someone who shared the same cultural and religious background. She raised questions and sought clarifications. The controlling, teasing, provocative, manipulative behavior engaged the analyst actively, eliciting reassurance and a structuring approach. It conveyed her problem with commitment and her intense anxiety and neediness; as a characteristic mode of coping with anxiety, it constituted the defense transference.

In the seventh session, she reported a dream vague in content, with a concern about being observed lying on the couch. A senior analyst was present, helping her analyst. She felt this must be his supervisor, relating it in her associations to her preoccupation with a father-brother couple. She expressed her fear of loss of control on the couch and touched on its sexual connotation for her. There were associated memories of having been forbidden to see certain T.V. shows by her father when she was a child and of a maid fixing her compensatory milkshakes. She presented this overstimulated and charged response to the onset of her analysis in a session in which she was 15 minutes late and sat on the couch for half an hour. After a session in which she reviewed her experience with girlfriends through the years, and her mother's intrusive interference with her choices, a tearful, depressive mood became evident. She sat in a chair throughout the hour. She complained that she felt like an adolescent exhibiting herself and recalled that at age 12 she had taken off her clothes in front of her uncle, and that he had almost "freaked out." She reported that sitting up was a "rebellion," like playing games with her brother. She liked being in control, but was afraid of being punished with termination of the analysis. The hostility and rebellion also had a flirtatious quality about it.

In this opening phase of the analysis, the patient revealed oedipal conflicts, unfinished mourning of her father and brother, and serious questions about the reliability of the analytic situation as a means of understanding her experiences. The anger at her mother's intrusive behavior and at the limits imposed by her father on what might be viewed and understood had obvious transference implications. The challenging, manipulative defense transference was a response to analytic experiences that heightened her anxiety, such as the analyst's acceptance of her for analysis, her first use of the couch, the emergence of conflict-laden material, etc. She complained about her difficulty in using the couch, and would sit up to maintain eye contact and confront the analyst with her disruption of the analytic ritual. She was attentive to realistic elements in the analytic setting, the furnishings and decorations, the analyst's speech, dress, and manner. The analyst's response was sympathetic and soothing. He acknowledged her anxiety and encouraged her participation in the process, permitting the rebellious behavior without being provoked.

Her need to see her analyst as a real person was strongly invested. In the 16th hour she brought a camera along and took his picture. The analyst viewed the defense transference as a "mirror transference," in which the patient sought visual contact with her mother as she engaged the task of mourning her father and brother. In the session preceding the camera episode, she revealed that the analyst reminded her of her brother but that his clothes seemed more like her father's. Interruptions in the analysis became an early and expectable focus of intense emotional reactions, with fear for the analyst's safety and bitter anger. The accident was paramount in her thoughts and fantasies.

The analyst felt that the patient needed to establish a sense of security in the maternal transference in order to engage and work through the traumatic neurosis initiated by the accident. He did not attempt active interpretations, but attended to her affective state—her fears of being left, excluded, without control or choice. As she experienced her bitterness and anger in mourning, she was enabled to confront her denial of the death of her father and brother and the illusion that the analyst represented them. This healing of the split in her ego permitted development of more of an "as if" quality in her transference reactions. The transference neurosis then flowered in more classical dimensions, and was interpreted. In the interest of economy, no detailed description of the analysis of her conflicts will be attempted. The patient's view of her experience will be noted in the follow-up interviews. Suffice it to say that she experienced and reported sexual fantasies in the father and brother transference, and analyzed her problems with femininity with respect to her tomboy behavior and her adolescent dilemma about identifying with a mother who was tough, independent, and quite conflicted about her own femininity. Homosexual regressive longings were also experienced and analyzed in the negative Oedipus complex.

Decision about Termination

As the patient began to confront the issue of termination, she regressed, feeling helpless and unable to do anything. In the analysis, she felt unable to associate to or understand her dreams, although she had become rather capable in this area. Her behavior was interpreted as a reaction to the threat of loss in that it repeated aspects of her experience after the loss of her father and brother. It also expressed penis envy and her rage at her mother for leaving her "incomplete and castrated." A cycle of oedipal conflicts ensued with fantasies more overt and clear. Provocative demanding questions and efforts to manipulate a response remained recurring keynotes, but now in more muted form. In the course of the analysis, these were repetitive phenomena, marking heightened tensions about oedipal conflicts and separations. The analyst interpreted their defensive function as the analysis proceeded, and gradually discontinued the mirroring responses and sympathetic permissiveness of the early period of the analysis. As she considered termination, she insisted on knowing why she had been accepted for analysis (fantasizing that she was special). She demanded repeated statements of an interpretation, and attempted to put her analyst on the spot about the issue of termination; it was his responsibility and not hers. She thought of bickering about a date, refusing to leave, etc. With renewed mourning, she reviewed the accident and her feelings of maternal abandonment in various transference manifestations. She finally set a date, six months later. She sought to experience a gradual termination, rather than the abrupt, traumatic experience of the past. After some analysis of the request, her analyst accepted it as appropriate, and agreed to see her for two months on a once-a-week basis at the end of the analysis.

Termination

In the final sessions of the analysis the defense transference was expressed in the form of challenging questions about an analytic colleague and other matters. The cycle of conflicts and the patient's acquired insights and analytic skills were also evident. In session #850, she reported a dream in which the analyst was criticizing her for biting her nails while his own five-year-old son was able to stop. She also pictured him as supporting his wife in the dream when his wife interviewed her as a patient. In her associations, she recognized her father's aloofness and her mother's inability to serve as a protector and a model for her. She recognized the resurgence of these conflicts in the transference and understood the wish to be a social friend as a defensive suppression of the conflicts as well as a desire to master them. In session #851, she reported a dream in which she was in a high-class dress shop trying on different dresses. The seamstress was supposed to shorten them. She found herself clumsy about tipping the seamstress. Her efforts to achieve some integration of her femininity were expressed in the dream. She forthrightly sought a style of dress congenial to her as a woman but revealed, in her clumsiness, a childlike clinging to mother. The problem in the dream about tipping was linked to what the fee would be for the once-a-week sessions in the final two months of her analysis as a special service provided by the analyst. This arrangement expressed in the transference the residuals of her dyadic conflicts in the last year. In the last hour, longing for her mother and anger were quite apparent. She fantasized arrangements for her analyst's wake (in association with the accident) as well as thoughts of fainting in the hour and thereby demanding attention. There was an accompanying fantasy of having a "therapist all her life," an effort to deny the loss of the analyst reminiscent of her attempt to deny her father's death. She reported, however, that these fantasies and feelings were limited to the analytic setting. Her life was coming along well, and she felt her sadness as appropriate to termination.

Follow-Up

Two years following termination, the patient was seen in a series of six follow-up interviews scheduled at weekly intervals. In the initial interview, the behavior we have described as the defense transference was immediately apparent in a barrage of questions about the follow-up analyst's credentials and the research. In the course of the interview, she described with laughter her own manipulative approach and voiced a teasing promise that it would become apparent in these interviews. Her awareness of her behavior was quite clear and its intensity and duration were much reduced in this initiation of the research alliance.

She reported that while introspection was natural to her and that she had thought about her analysis in response to the exchange of letters setting up the follow-up interviews, there had been a diminution in deliberate self-analytic efforts after termination. In the course of her analysis, she had kept a diary in which she had noted her dreams, but she had not returned to review them and had stopped keeping any record of her dreams after the analysis was over. She supposed that there was not the same reward system to reinforce recall and analysis. She gave an excellent resumé of her analytic experience. She described the first two years as occupied with mourning the loss of her father and brother, and regarded this experience as critical to her further development. The last two years of her analysis were involved with her sexual feelings and her problems with femininity and competition. She had gained from the analysis the tools to understand herself. Her platonic relationship with the older married man had continued after the analysis, and she had been accepted into his family like another daughter. Some two months prior to the follow-up, the wife of her friend had died, creating the conditions for an oedipal triumph. The relationship had quickly changed from platonic to sexual. She said with ironic amusement that her experience contradicted the need for renunciation of her wishes and wondered what Freud would have to say about that. In reviewing her analysis, she reported that the efforts to understand her sexual feelings had not freed her to have an orgasm and that she still feared such a release. She had sought out thrills for her sexual pleasure, but without any real risk of commitment. Her career as a musician had been marked with some success, but she still had difficulty in being as productive as she would have liked. As she registered these complaints about the unfinished business of her analysis, she recalled that her analyst had interpreted similar complaints about her persistent problems as manipulative devices which she used to avoid dealing with the threat of separation and its traumatic associations.

In the second interview, she was more composed and distant. She recognized that the follow-up analyst was a stranger, and was concerned about issues of loyalty to her analyst. The "stranger" feeling was heightened when her fantasy that the follow-up analyst was her analyst's supervisor was shattered by his answer to her direct question that he was not. She expressed much disappointment. The difficulty this created for her with regard to committing herself to the follow-up research was acknowledged by the analyst, and his sympathetic response was greeted with a smile and a renewed interest in the interviews. When her fantasy was questioned, she recognized the recurrence of her pleasurable preoccupation with the father-brother theme in its supervisor-analyst version. She recalled, with some confusion about the time, the end of her analysis, and how she had had to face the fact that it was really over and her life was in her hands. The two months of once-a-week visits had been a delaying tactic, expressing her reluctance to leave, in spite of all the work that had been done on issues of separation. With regard to the further fate of the alliance, she reported that she had found a woman friend completing her own analysis with whom she had engaged in some mutual analytic conversation. Her friend was unlike her, and readily distinguishable as a separate person, a good friend, like the older sister she never had. She told her friend about her trouble with having orgasms, so that she would not be jealous of her relationships with men. While she made no concerted effort to understand herself, she would find herself applying in her daily life what she had learned from her analysis (she was, for example, able to follow trains of association in conversation and make illuminating inferences that helped her with associates and friends). On such occasions she sometimes thought of how pleased her analyst would be with her proficiency. She reported a continued interest in the real life of her analyst whenever she met anyone who knew him. His benign presence in her thoughts was apparent.

In the third interview, the defense transference appeared in a more intense burst of activity. After some comments about her appreciation of the visits and her good vibes about them, she returned to the provocative, challenging, teasing behavior that revived almost exactly in content and form her behavior early in the analysis. She questioned whether the follow-up analyst was Jewish, and elaborated the significance of that question for her. She questioned why there were six interviews. Was it all ritualized? What if she had more to reveal and six were not enough? The follow-up analyst focused on her concern about how well she could be understood and whether the visits were mechanical and arbitrary. She said that these same problems arose in all her relationships, and related her concerns about her proficiency in verbal communication. (These concerns were striking in their contradiction of reality because her verbal skills in the follow-up interviews were excellent.) In elaborating the reasons why she needed a Jewish analyst, whose life experience would enable him to fill in deficiencies in her account, she reported that her intellectual abilities had gone quite unrecognized in her family. Her ineptitude was stressed by her mother in all things academic. When she was described by her platonic friend as a bright and clever girl, her mother was quite surprised. Her activities as a musician were depreciated by her mother and aunt, who asked a friend to evaluate her playing, as though even in musical form her ability to communicate was a surprise to them. She recalled an incident in grammar school when she had been flunking and had worked furiously to avoid having to go to summer school. She had achieved the top grade in the course, but it had been a triumph that she did not repeat. She characterized herself as spacy and daydreamy. The follow-up analyst questioned what prompted her to persist in such behavior when she had demonstrated her ability on the exam. She recognized that her balking, provocative school behavior had been a means of engaging her mother's attention. Her mother had been called to school, to talk to teachers and to worry about homework and grades. Consistently in the past as in the present, her behavior had expressed a wish to be exceptional in her own way, to dramatize herself and break out of the confines of expectable behavior in her interactions with people. She gave as an example the regimentation of the interview. If she accepted the way it was, she was unexceptional. Thus, she liked to engage in rebel games, to break with the methods people normally used. She liked to win and do it her way. The follow-up analyst reminded her of her description of herself as a manipulator and how it would become evident in these interviews. She reacted with surprise and then with amused recognition and a reflective mood. She recalled how in her analysis she would not lie down on the couch for some time. It had been a contest with her analyst to see when the necessity to lie down would be enforced. The follow-up analyst underlined the fact that it was not just fear, but game playing that had motivated her behavior. She had thought it a way of cracking her analyst's professional incognito, to get him to respond personally. She went on to describe how the game had been played out in the sexual arena with her analyst. She thought of her sexual experiences as organic and synthetic. The organic was repressed. She was very inhibited sexually. In the analysis she had tried to simulate sexual experience in her thoughts and fantasies. She elaborated on her basic identification in this area with her mother. She recalled her mother's brief remarriage after the accident. Her stepfather had given her mother a book of passionate poems. Her mother had found her reading it, and in a panic had wrenched it from her and thrown it against the wall. She noted what a poor model her mother had provided for her in adolescence, and recalled her tomboyish behavior at age four or five.

In this informative exchange, the defense transference was revealed as a form of pseudo-autonomy, a manipulative, rebellious, provocative expression of her original approach to the world, one that would crack the conventional mold. The confusion about dates and historical detail in her memories testified to an ability to adapt reality in such a way as to limit her encounter with conflict. The "simulated" conflicts introduced into the analytic process indicated that there was a gamelike quality to the experience for her. Pleasure in the game combined with its defensive value in holding reality at bay. As a musician, she fashioned reality to her own measure in a sublimated form which emphasized its adaptive potential. Her creativity set limits to the solution of intrapsychic conflict in her own life. Though the defense transference was couched, in this interview, in the context of latency experience and its repetition in the analytic process, its earlier roots in separation-individuation became apparent and were elaborated in some further details adduced in subsequent interviews.

The fourth session opened with another skirmish in the defense transference. There was a salvo of questions about the conclusions reached in follow-up research and about the outcome of analysis. The follow-up analyst calmly suggested that their purposes would better be served by exploring her own analytic experience. With the mutual recognition of her mode of relating, she turned seriously to the work at hand. She had thought of the accident in the perspective of her whole life and had decided it simply added complications to her identity and her sexual behavior. One of the important issues in her life had been her relationship with her older brother. He had had the position of honor and respect in the family and she had idolized him. She had attributed his favored position entirely to the difference in their sexes, disregarding the prerogatives that accrued to him because of age. She had developed the tactic of rebellion in competition with him for their mother's attention. At the age of two, she had become quite competitive with her brother. She had changed the color of her room from pink to blue and been intentionally sloppy. Mother had typically responded to her rebelliousness by pretending it was not important and that she didn't care. But this attempt to undermine her rebellion had failed. It had simply led to an escalation of her efforts to force mother to respond (as when the mother had been called to school). In adolescence, her problems with her femininity had been accentuated. After the accident, her mother had encouraged eating as a form of gratification, and they had both struggled with obesity. She had taken no interest in her hair and appearance and had expressed herself in the form of a distorted exhibitionism, as in the episode with her uncle at age 12. In her current view of herself, she dressed in the style of musicians generally, with attention to her hair and appearance. She accepted herself and her struggle, and chose friends who were more appropriate models. Their responses to her increased her self-assurance with regard to her femininity. She described an active effort to meet men and to struggle with her problems with intimacy and sex. She felt that she had to take risks and be open to experience because of her wish to get married and have a child. She began to talk about the complexities in the relationship with her mentor and lover now that his wife had died.

In the fifth interview, she pursued a discussion of the relationship, pointing out its realistic problems due to differences in age, outlook, and friends. A note of volatile bickering had entered their relationship along with the sex. She had felt her independence, her style and character, threatened, yet the relationship was also intensely important to her. The conflict-laden aspects were acute. She had not recognized her guilt about the death of his wife as a significant ingredient in her reactions. When asked about her use of dreams and fantasies in understanding her current stress, she said that she did not use them much, and yet recalled that recent dreams had had to do with her mother and that in considering looking for a home with her lover she had somehow cast him in a maternal role. She described the function of the defense transference in the game she played with her lover, a game in which she used the same technique of provocative questioning and manipulation. She described herself as a gameperson. She loved games. She laughed and said they offered a time-out from life. Toward the end of the fifth interview the follow-up analyst suggested the possibility that feelings of guilt might be disrupting her loving relationship and prompting her to cast herself in a childlike role with a mothering person. He also related a depressive mood (which she had noted and described in the session) to the approaching termination of the follow-up sessions. She hesitantly acknowledged the possibility of guilt feelings and her need to retain comforting ties with her mother. The depression about the end of the sessions was now more apparent to her.

She postponed the final meeting of the follow-up a week because of a trip she had planned, thereby expressing her reluctance to finish just as she had in her analysis.

In the last session she reported a dream in which a radio repairman, in a setting like that of a short-order cook, does not have her radio ready. In the same dream, she passes an automobile accident. At first she is an observer and then she comes to be represented both as the driver of the car and as one of two pedestrians who were trying to separate and were then hit by the car. Her struggle with mourning and conflict in her relationship with her lover was repeated in the transference context of the follow-up. She presented the dream with a comment that she was responding to the question about her use of dreams in understanding herself, as though to satisfy a request made by the follow-up analyst. She did some effective work in associating to the dream, but expressed her view that she could not have understood it by herself in the same way. Her mourning response, anger, and guilt were actively engaged in the process. The setting of the follow-up at a time when she was responding to very dramatic changes in her life, and the intensification of oedipal conflicts and mourning it had brought about, lent a note of urgency and distress to the experience, bringing the defense transference into still clearer focus. The depreciation of her own intellect and self-analytic capacity was similar to her behavior in school, and pointed to the significance of her conflict over separation-individuation in determining the nature of the defense transference. Just as her childhood difficulties in school had been designed to attract her mother's attention, thereby to restore the harmony of the dyadic relationship (a relationship constantly undermined, in her experience, by her brother's own demands for attention), so too did she "fail" now at self-analysis in order to re-engage the analyst in the analytic dyad. Similarly, her characteristic patterns of behavior—pleasurable gameplaying and musical accomplishment—remained rooted in the need to engage her mother's attention. The problem in separating and the threatening nature of separating were both captured in the dream image of the two pedestrians trying to disengage, and then being struck by the car.

We would regard this pattern of behavior, so consistently and repetitively evident in this patient's analysis and follow-up, as the outcome of her separation-individuation experience. The rebellious, provocative mode, forcing attention and response from her mother, was first evidenced at the age of two in her competitiveness with her brother and her sloppiness. Latency-age manifestations included her tomboyishness, her school behavior, and her struggle with oedipal conflicts. The pattern was effective with her mother and effectively endorsed by her participation in it. It is an interesting fact, reported by the patient, that her mother was an excellent gameplayer, very proficient at a variety of table games. Thus, identification with the mother served as the basis for the defense transference pattern itself. While the defense transference was within the awareness of the patient in analysis and at follow-up, and was interpreted as a defense and understood to some extent, its modification in analysis was limited. Its containment was dependent on the benign and soothing responses of her analyst and of the friends she sought out after termination—precisely the kind of psychotherapeutic "interventions" we described in Chapter 4. In this area of the analytic alliance, then, the defense transference was not actively analyzed with respect to its earliest precursors. The analytic process was effectively replaced by a psychotherapeutic process in such a way that the full transference potential of the analyst-patient relationship could not be realized, nor could any attempt be made to influence the patient's patterns of behavior by reconstruction and transmuting internalization. As a hopeful denouement, we should report that the patient returned to her analyst for some further work on her problems after the follow-up interviews.

Discussion

From the beginning of our follow-up studies the defense transference has been a significant focus of our attention in the assessment of change. What we have described in detail in the preceding case has been corroborated by our experience generally. We typically found that the pattern of behavior we designated the defense transference came into play whenever a conflictual area was engaged in the cycles of conflict that constitute the analytic process. It was modified in duration and intensity as the cycles speeded up and as conflicts increasingly came to be observed, tolerated, and integrated by the patient. The defense transference was usually identified and interpreted by the analyst as a regressive defense against oedipal conflict, so as to facilitate the appearance of the transference neurosis and the analysis of its conflicts. We have emphasized earlier that the psychoanalytic situation and the analyst's exquisite attention to the patient may have a therapeutic effect on early developmental problems imbricated in the analytic alliance and that, indeed, the analyst's effort to elicit the transference neurosis often has a structuring effect. The degree to which problems in the defense transference itself are subjected to analysis varies. Certainly the problems are identified, and they may be related to the early family setting, but they are given a subsidiary role and regarded as evidence of resistance to the "real" analytic effort.

In the follow-up interviews, the defense transference reappeared as the cycle of conflicts was repeated. The follow-up interviews were regarded as similar to a renewal of the analysis or a refresher course in which the follow-up analyst was readily cast in a familiar role. In the post-analytic life of the analysands generally, the frequently observed effort to establish a friend or a spouse as an analytic surrogate or to remember the analytic experience in the face of emotional turmoil suggested the therapeutic efficacy and significance of the analytic situation in promoting a self-analytic function for the solution of neurotic conflict. Former patients experienced the defense transference as a familiar phenomenon in their own self-observation, and recalled its presence in their analyses, often ruefully as a disruptive influence, sometimes humorously with a note of transformed narcissism. These modifications in the defense transference were significant achievements. In one instance, a patient whose characteristic defense had been a retreat into helplessness, thereby to mobilize a rescue by parental surrogates, described a new post-analytic version of the defense, a form of brinksmanship, in which she would display helplessness and then surprise everyone with her ability to rescue herself. She delighted in creating such surprises. The adaptive repertoire of the patients had generally been enriched by their awareness of the defense transference and its management.

Limitations in the analysis of the defense transference were quite common, however, and often glaring in their import. In some patients, as reported in Chapter 4, the problems evident at follow-up demonstrated that the analytic solutions were, to a significant extent, incorporated in the defense transference mode (in compliance, a wish to please, a need for premature mastery, as an intellectual solution, etc.). The problems in tension regulation remained, and constituted a threat to the accomplishments of the analysis. The defense transference had not been addressed as a specific focus of analytic interest, deserving of analysis in its own right. Because of the adaptive

usefulness of the defense transference and the psychotherapeutic effects of the analytic situation, problems in
separation-individuation were obscured or simply interpreted in their defensive function. Such problems became
more poignant in the termination phase with the contemplation of a complete separation, revealing their pathological effects in a defective self-soothing function, based
on defects in self-object differentiation and reality processing. In the termination phase, in conjunction with
the actively recurring cycles of conflict involved in the
transference neurosis, there was consolidation of the development of ego functions in a kind of reworking of separation-individuation. In this active process, tension-
regulatory modes may be altered by means of reconstruction and understanding of the past and through the internalizations that occur in connection with the
management of the patient's tensions by the analyst. The
fact that the resumption of the real relationship can no
longer be anticipated increases the intensity of old separation-individuation problems. The manifestations of
these problems demand analysis rather than simple identification, confrontation, and denigration as defensive. In
our case examples in Chapter 6, we shall illustrate such
a change in focus in analytic processes that had regarded
characterological behavior merely as a defense against
oedipal conflict. The careful analytic investigation of such
"mere defensive behavior" may lead to the dramatic repetition of derivatives of separation-individuation and the
possibility of re-solution of early conflicts in object relations.

Chapter 6

Tension Regulation in the Development of a Self-Analytic Function

Our research findings and clinical experiences have convinced us of the importance of analytic attention to tension-regulatory functions that antedate oedipal conflicts and are essentially experienced in a dyadic context as a part of the analytic process. In our view, the self-analytic capacities stemming from analysis of the special configuration of the Oedipus complex may be seriously compromised by a lack of adequate attention to these modes of tension regulation. To repeat, it is particularly in the termination phase of an analysis and its aftermath in later developmental crises that problems with self-soothing in the context of separation become most acute, especially where such problems have been regarded and interpreted merely as regressive defensive phenomena earlier in the analysis, when psychoneurotic conflicts took center stage. Continued neglect of such early developmental determinants may contribute to a situation in which the self-analytic function is built on shifting sands and the beneficial outcome of the analytic process is put at risk. In this chapter we shall cite illustrative clinical examples supporting this view in anecdotal material from first and second analyses that contributed to and benefited from the insights gained in this research effort.

The case example reviewed in Chapter 2 (case 1) illustrates our thesis very well. The first analysis of this young woman was directed at psychoneurotic features in an oedipal paradigm and resulted in significant changes in her primary concern about relating to men and the general insecurity that prompted her entry into analysis. She had required a structuring, supportive approach from her analyst to manage her potential for irritating nagging dependence and her intense screaming and provocative behavior. The analyst conveyed an empathic comprehension of her anxiety, encouraged her to observe it, and provided hope that insight could make it more manageable. The structuring activity of the analyst was clearly evident at termination. Shortly after the analysis was concluded, her mother died. The patient utilized her self-analytic skills and a return visit to her analyst to mourn effectively and to recover a positive identification with some of the more admirable aspects of her alcoholic mother's character. Changes in her feminine identification and her object choices permitted her to make a successful marriage. Her husband's benign support contrasted with the troubled relationships with men she had experienced in the past and helped her to maintain a reasonable adaptation.

The abrupt death of her father complicated her pregnancy and was particularly hard to bear because of the emotional upheaval he had suffered in his terminal illness. The problems she experienced in modulating her infant's needs for soothing and for maternal care served to disrupt her adaptive solution and to bring into focus incomplete aspects of her analysis. Her tense screaming behavior and heightened inability to participate in an analytic alliance was addressed by the second analyst in another context from that of a defense against oedipal conflict. The recovered knowledge of her infantile eczema, which had necessitated binding her to her crib and had been accompanied by incessant screaming and crying in the early months of her life, was a dramatic keynote related to other evidence of early deprivation in maternal solicitude and attention. Her characteristic pattern of relating to her mother had involved containment, an external set of limits to control rising tensions of whatever variety under stress. Once her agitated complaining had engaged her mother's attention she would receive further structure and reassurance to the point that things were once again "okay." Her first analyst had provided such a structuring response in stilling her agitation while he pursued his interpretive approach to her psychoneurotic conflicts. In effect, he had accepted and participated in her adaptive solution to dyadic problems. The patient had herself set limits to the analytic effort by her determination to complete the analysis in three years.

In the second analysis, the dyadic problems were no longer avoidable. As she attempted to be a mother for her first child, her own tension-regulatory functions were severely taxed and she displayed her problems to her analyst in startling intensity. She sought controls and limits from him but was met with an effort to truly understand the early developmental determinants of her experience. Once the memories about her early eczema were recovered and some beginning reconstructions of her early experiences were conveyed to her, a working alliance could be established so as to enable her to explore the repetition in the analytic situation of narcissistic transferences and separation-individuation experiences. Expectations of maternal rejection, the wish for mirroring responses, and rage at any separation or lack of understanding on the part of the analyst were an ongoing focus of the process of discovery. Confrontations with disavowed aspects of herself were particularly painful in the renewed effort to utilize her analyst as a selfobject, reconstructing the traumatic aspects of the past and internalizing functions of protective attention and understanding. Early identifications with her mother were evident in her own efforts to mother her child, in the form of threatening mortification and rage at her incapacities as a mother and her needs as a child. The artificial limits on the analytic effort were relinquished as the patient learned that there was a prospect of being herself, knowing her own feelings and wishes, and establishing her own direction rather than accommodating to expectations and a rigid program for living. As she was better able to respond to her children's needs, her own self-soothing capabilities improved. The changes wrought in this dyadic sphere were evident in improved reality processing, self-object differentiation, and the tolerance and mastery of frustration, anxiety, and depression, creating a more secure base for her self-analytic capacity and securing the gains in her ability to deal with neurotic conflicts.

The follow-up cited in Chapter 3 (Case 2) demonstrates in a similar way the significance of tension regulation in a dyadic context. The patient had entered her first analysis at age 25 as a graduate student in professional school, complaining of frustrating, self-destructive relationships with men and problems with supervisors at work. Her characterological armor was a brusque, disdainful attitude mobilized by anxiety-provoking situations. When this defensive attitude was modified, cyclic conflicts were evident in dyadic concerns about maternal nurture tinged with latent homosexual elements and followed by heterosexual problems involving an unwitting choice of men as maternal substitutes and a failure to enjoy sex. The repetition of the conflicts in analysis and their analytic comprehension and working through was reflected in the development of a self-analytic capacity, demonstrated in her marriage, in her mourning of the deaths of her brother and mother post-analytically, and in her behavior in the follow-up sessions. Residual problems were noted in her use of her husband as a maternal controlling figure to regulate tensions when her anxiety mounted (albeit with subsequent self-scrutiny) and in some limitations in confronting derivatives of oedipal conflicts.

The patient returned for further analysis some four years after termination. As in the preceding case, the precipitating factor was a problem in mothering. She struggled with the need to wean her child and was unenthusiastic about sex. Her brusque, disdainful, critical attitude entered into the second analysis in a new context, related to an underlying depression and a second look at early deprivation and distortion in her relationship with her mother. Her conflict about giving up nursing was traced to these roots. When she pressed for rapid closure based on this explanation, her analyst noted the need for further work on her depression. She felt hurt and depreciated, became brusque and cold, and revealed her need to demonstrate that she was whole and well. Her narcissistic vulnerability was related to a sense of defectiveness which had been attributed to penis envy in the first analysis. In this renewed effort to explore the origins of her feelings of despair and worthlessness, her own unwitting abrupt and critical attitudes became clear as an effort to maintain an invulnerable, arrogant posture. Her needs had to be controlled by her characterological façade and she thereby lost the friendly interest she desired so much.

In attempting to handle her daughter's reaction to the birth of a second child, her intolerance for a range of feelings in the mother-child relationship became the center of analytic interest. When her daughter expressed hurt and disappointment and turned to a neighbor for solace, the patient withdrew into melancholy and helplessness, fearing her own rage. The analysis then proceeded with an investigation and unravelling of the patient's problems with separation-individuation. Her mother had not felt good about herself, escaping into a busy preoccupation with community efforts, offering a model for such a solution to the child struggling with yearnings for nurture, attention, and approval. Tension regulation was maintained by means of disavowal and suppression and the controlling characterological features of brusqueness, coldness, and self-sufficiency. The second analysis in no way vitiated the explanations and symbolic meanings of psychoneurotic symptoms arrived at in the first analysis. It uncovered, rather, an infrastructure of tension-regulatory problems and their characterological solution, one rooted in a basic identification with the mother. Its modification rested on a working through of memories and transferences from the separation-individuation era as they entered the analytic process.

The analysis of the three supervised cases reported below occurred concomitantly with our follow-up studies. Insights gained in the research influenced their conduct, particularly at termination. These case reports therefore illustrate in clinical form the consequences of the research in heightened attention to dyadic problems with tension regulation.

CASE 5

The following case vignette illustrates the use of fantasy in a simultaneous solution of oedipal conflict and separation-individuation conflicts. The patient was a 30-year-old woman with a recurring pattern of involvements with married men that inevitably ended in sad frustration and were marked by frigidity in sexual experiences. The hysterical features suggested by the presenting complaints were borne out in analysis. Her behavior was recognized and interpreted as the acting out of oedipal rivalry with her mother. The affairs had also served to excite her mother's attention and concern. The transference roots in analytic day residue were unearthed with difficulty early in the analysis. Frustrated fantasies were inferred from the patient's bitter anger and recriminations. The analytic effort to explore and identify the fantasies was experienced as similar to mother's intrusive interest in her romantic affairs. Married men were like pawns in her acting out, her affairs with them demonstrating repetitively her ability to win her father. The significance of the pattern became increasingly apparent and gradually developed a convincing transference coloration that could be identified in her dreams and analytic experiences.

The termination phase, however, proved to be protracted and difficult. Repetition of the interpretive effort directed at oedipal material had little effect. The fantasies persisted and the patient expressed a sense of conviction about them that raised questions about her ability to differentiate reality from fantasy.

The delineation of the dyadic meanings of her use of fantasy followed on a shift in the analyst's comprehension of the problem and a change in technique. It became apparent that the continued interpretations of the fantasies as efforts to deal with oedipal conflict did not yield more than a reluctant acknowledgment that the conflicts were still there. The interpretations were accompanied by feelings of humiliation and tentative concern about separation. The patient experienced her humiliation as following from an intentional shaming act of the analyst, with a degree of conviction that testified to the significance of the experience for her. The reduction of this intense transference reaction was therefore a key to analyzing the early origins of her defensive use of fantasy. Efforts to deal with her fears of humiliation had of course been made throughout her analysis and had been successful enough to expose the oedipal configuration to interpretation. In the context of separation-individuation, shame and humiliation had an even stronger valence. Confrontation of the issue and interpretive and reconstructive efforts resulted in some relief and in a substantial strengthening of the analytic alliance, and set the stage for risking the recapitulation of early developmental traumata in memory, imagery, and action.

The course of separation-individuation had been disrupted for this patient by the arrival of a younger brother when she was two years old. The brother had been favored by both parents. She had suffered a temporary regression with his arrival and with her consignment to another room in the house, removed from the nursery and parental attention. Her language acquisition and toilet training had been temporarily disrupted. Sibling rivalry with fear of her own rage had contributed to problems in consolidating object constancy as well as to a narcissistic vulnerability about her femininity. There had been a heavy reliance on transitional objects to relieve anxiety about separation. Her interest in dolls and stuffed animals (which had persisted into adult life) had gradually shifted to a use of fantasy as a kind of intrapsychic tran-

sitional object. Her mother had been inordinately interested in her fantasies and secrets to the point that she
had almost sought to inhabit the same skin with her
daughter in a symbiotic-like tie, reflecting the mother's
lifelong difficulty in separating from her own mother.
The investment in fantasy had been reinforced by the
mother's delight in treating the patient's fantasies as
though they were real and her subsequently reporting
them to friends with great amusement. Mother's constant
interest had served as a reliable object tie, albeit tinged
with the prospect of humiliation. Reality processing had
been endangered thereby and a primary process mode of
thought encouraged. The patient's use of fantasies was
thus the consequence of a developmental distortion of the
normal course of reality processing that served a tension-
regulatory function in managing separation problems,
and that later came to influence the patient's response
to developmentally subsequent conflicts, including oedipal conflicts. This developmental distortion and neurotic
conflict coexisted in her psychopathology.

The use of fantasy in the analytic process first became
evident as a symptom in her response to the analyst's
efforts to understand her experiences. Any analytic interest in fantasy was pleasurable to her but rapidly became tinged with anxiety. Tension states were aroused
when she recognized that reality did not coincide with
her fantasies. These reactions were understood only when
the special significance of fantasy in her experience of
separation-individuation was identified. Efforts at empathy or inferences drawn from her associations were
experienced as a threatening disruption of a symbiotic
state with further anxiety about subsequent revelations.
To relinquish her use of fantasy exposed her not only to
the loss of her solution to oedipal conflict but also to the
unfinished business of separation-individuation—her

problems with self-object differentiation and reality processing. The inability to tolerate and master her own
affects and impulses was expressed in actual neurotic
symptomatology. Analysis of her patterns of behavior and
reconstruction of its origins served to foster the development of structure requisite for independent, realistic
problem solving.

CASE 6

The patient was a young graduate student at a local
university, the only son of immigrant parents. His presenting complaint was a problem with completing his
thesis in philosophy, an endeavor which had undermined
his confidence and caused him to question what he had
really learned in his studies. His mother was a histrionic,
intelligent, somewhat superstitious woman who was intensely invested in her son. From an early age he had
demonstrated superior qualities of intellect and the rapid
acquisition of motor and verbal skills. His accelerated
development further excited his mother's hopes and ambitions for him and he experienced her admiration with
pleasure and joined her in fantasies of greatness. The
impetus for fulfillment of his ambitious strivings was
further strengthened by her reaction to his father's struggle to maintain a small grocery business that offered little
more than the bare necessities in return for long and
tedious labor. His mother attached all her frustrated
hopes to the patient with unbounded expectations. In
spite of the high level of his competence, the intensity of
her demand led to a need for instant mastery and a counterphobic exploration of life beyond the limits that constricted the lives of his parents.

His analysis unfolded rapidly. There was a strong oedipal cast to the presenting material. In the special con-

figurations of the Oedipus complex, his grandiose ambitions predictably involved the displacement of his depreciated father and a wish to become all that his mother might desire. Fears of his competitiveness were hypertrophied in correspondence to the intensity of his desires. His fantasy life was rich and imaginative and permitted a useful exposition of his conflicts. Elements of inhibition in his work and in his relationships with women were addressed as intrapsychic conflicts, with the recovery of memories of overstimulated states with mother and fearful competitive fantasies involving father. The negative Oedipus complex unfolded as well with a longing for a strong father who would help control his impulses and provide for his suppressed childlike desires.

In spite of achievements in his work consistent with his considerable abilities, he was severely hampered by the very intensity of his desire for success. Phobic elements in his character exercised a limiting effect on the integration of what he had learned and there was a tendency to overcome them with a display of mastery that was not securely based, so that he felt his intellectual acquisitions as a mosaic of knowledge. Underlying his grandiose fantasies, he felt like an impostor. The difficulties in pursuing his work included occasional bursts of concern about his physical condition, centering on his bowel functions, an area of great interest to his mother who had amply conveyed her frequent preoccupation with her own bowels. The mother's overprotective interest in his bowels was quite at odds with her usual exaggerated expectations in his childhood. His childhood illnesses were islands of maternal solicitude in a turbulent sea of maternal demands.

While specific fantasies, dreams, and transference reactions were analyzable with the stellar participation of the patient, there was a lack of continuity in the process;

something of the mosaic of knowledge that characterized the patient's learning in school seemed to be repeated in his analysis. Nevertheless, the analytic effort was accompanied by a reduction in anxiety, improved functioning in his work and in social relationships, and a pressure to terminate. At this juncture, even though he pressed to finish, he reluctantly acknowledged an increased preoccupation with his bowels, and his dreams belied the profession of confidence in his ability to cope with his problems. He began an affair with a young secretary whose race and general interests were at variance with his own. The effort to understand his somatic concerns as regressive and/or self-punitive had little effect. The interpretation of his choice of a woman so unlike his mother as an alleviation of oedipal conflict met with no greater success.

Just as in the previous case, the explanation of the patient's psychological state at this point in the analysis shifted toward his problems with tension regulation. In his choice of a girlfriend, he had found someone who shared his mother's admiration for him but did not assault him with exaggerated expectations. For her, he could do no wrong. The preoccupation with his bowels represented a use of illness to still the tormenting maternal critic within him, whose expectations could be reduced only in a merger based on their common somatic complaints. Behavior that might have been interpreted as a regression from oedipal conflict was explored as a repetition of earlier developmental issues in separation-individuation. Intense affects and impulses, overstimulated states that threatened him with a loss of control, led to a reliance on illness and a pursuit of medical attention for reassurance, repeating the early anxious concerns of his mother. His desire was for an indulgent and self-sacrificial protector. In his pursuit of learning and in his usual relationships with women, his characterological mode served to assure compliance with his mother's expectations—in premature mastery, a counterphobic display of confidence, and a poorly integrated grasp of what he confronted in the world and in himself. In the course of the analytic work, the patient understood the nature of his task in terms of a need to integrate and make a part of himself the knowledge, skills, affects, and fantasies that had previously had a primarily adaptive function for him in appeasing harsh internal demands, hostile introjects, and authorities who appeared as threatening taskmasters.

Just as somatic preoccupations had served a wish for symbiotic union with mother and the desire for a magical protector, so too did the analyst's comforting presence and efforts at understanding serve a similar purpose. Apart from their communicative value, words and explanations could be a comforting bond between analyst and patient. In analyzing the patient's use of the analyst for comfort and symbiotic union, the analyst made possible a renewed approach to individuation in a time frame appropriate to the patient's needs. Memories, feelings, and fantasies served the reconstruction of the patient's early experiences with overstimulated states and exaggerated expectations. Affects and impulses were subject to self-control when they were experienced as a part of the self and not accepted in compliance with some external view of them. Interpretation and insight were actively integrated, not merely passively accepted.

The analysis of oedipal conflict alone in this case, even with the analysis of pregenital regressive components, would have resulted in a termination in which the continued maintenance of the defense transference threatened the consolidation of self-analytic skills acquired in the process. The problems of tension regulation and capacity for self-soothing, as they came sharply into focus in the termination phase, required attention and analysis in their own right. The underpinnings of the analytic alliance demanded analytic scrutiny and appropriate intervention. A greater capacity for tension regulation offered a more secure basis for self-soothing and self-analysis.

CASE 7

For the last case in this series, we shall cite a patient whose follow-up consisted of a second analysis. In this analysis, as in Case 5, the focus was on the interplay between fantasy and reality in the dyadic frame of reference.

The patient, a 30-year-old woman and the only child of a middle-class family, came to analysis because of recurrent depression associated with feelings of inadequacy as a wife and dissatisfaction in her social relationships. Though obviously much admired by her husband and friends, she experienced these relationships as not affording her the pleasures and comforts she sought but rather as leaving her with feelings of emptiness and uneasiness. Her reactions seemed to be reflections of low self-esteem, though this was not immediately apparent in her dress, manner, and general interests in cultural and social events.

The father, a physician, had been much involved in establishing his practice in the first two years of her life and had then left for three years of army service, returning home when she was five years of age. The mother, described as a caring, nurturing woman, had been overly concerned with her only child, feeling that she had to make up to the child for the absence of a father in the home. The early memories of the patient were of a shared life of fantasy, an intense relationship with the mother in which the presence of the father was conjured up at fancied celebrations and parties. In these games, the child was the ostensible center of attention. For the mother, the child served as a narcissistic extension of herself and, in a sense, as a substitute for the absent father. The child readily complied in rituals that helped control anxiety about the absent father and soothed mother and child. In the parties, games, and fantasies, it was as if the father were an active participant in the scene.

Early in the first analysis, an apparently effective alliance was established and the special configuration of the Oedipus complex emerged. The ambivalence in the father transference was experienced and understood with regard to its many determinants. The father had been busy establishing his practice and had not had time for her; Army service had been further evidence of his un-availability, if not his outright desertion. Furthermore, the father's frustrated desire for a son with whom he could participate in masculine activities had become apparent to her on his return. As she grew up, he had not appreciated or encouraged her feminine aspirations. Her penis envy was heightened by the mother's obvious preoc-cupation with her father. In her own relationship with her husband, she tried to be very special to him and he was able to respond to some degree, but her longstanding frustration and bitterness could not easily be assuaged. She simultaneously sought in her husband a supportive, admiring, and loving male and a soothing, nurturing, attentive mother.

In the transference to the analyst, she wished for a similar special relationship. As the work of analysis pro-ceeded, rage emerged at the father for his unavailability and distance and at the mother for being a rival who was somehow responsible for sending father away or who was not adequate to keep him. Conflicts emerged most intensely at times of separation. Weekend separations were experienced over a long period of time as reenactments of the oedipal drama in which the analyst was cast as the absent, deserting, and rejecting father and the husband was expected to act as a nurturing replacement for the analyst. She expected him to provide entertainment and soothing affection and (like mother in the past) to participate in shopping sprees as a healing balm for the fantasied princess whose love for the charming prince went unrequited. Invariably, the frustrations mobilized in such situations led to raging, violent arguments in which the patient accused her husband of not caring, of having a roving eye, and of longing to be unfaithful. Interpretation of the displacements involved in this weekend behavior was acceptable and interesting to the patient. Though the frequency and intensity of the scenes were reduced, they persisted throughout most of the analysis.

On vacations, a somewhat more complicated pattern of behavior emerged. In whatever group they travelled, the patient would attach herself to the leader, the tour guide, the captain of the cruise ship, or the most attractive male. She would be the adoring admirer of this man and would spin a fantasy in which he could not resist her charms. She would be his out-and-out favorite, a brilliant star, and he would want her to be his companion and future wife. The end of the vacation was experienced as a traumatic dissolution of the fantasy, with a shocking reentry into the world of analysis. Only through analysis of the fantasy nature of her experience and its defensive function of protecting her from separation from her analyst could any inroads be made in the transference neurosis. In the transference, she harbored the illusion that she was the analyst's favorite patient and that, behind his façade, the analyst was secretly in love with her and some day would leave his wife for her. Persistent analytic exploration yielded negative oedipal material as well, in the jealous reactions she experienced with her husband and her analyst.

At the time of termination, there were many indications that pointed to a sustained decrease in the recurrent rageful attacks at times of separation. There seemed to be a more accurate perception of the men in her life and a more realistic orientation toward her own expectations. The shopping sprees had lost much of their urgency. The need for an elaborate wardrobe had been modified to such a degree that she could reasonably purchase what she desired. In addition, there seemed to be evidence of a sound self-analytic function in her ability to observe and understand her own reactions and explain them within the oedipal paradigm. The prospect of termination was pursued with a surprising degree of equanimity as well as some evidence of mourning. All of this indicated to the analyst that termination was appropriate and that the post-analytic phase of mourning would probably be well tolerated.

Approximately one year after termination, the patient returned for a consultation. She was quite depressed and expressed rageful feelings toward the analyst about unfulfilled promises. The need for further analysis seemed pressing, and analysis was resumed. Shortly after resumption of the analysis, the true nature of the termination phase was revealed. The patient had learned of her analyst's hobby—gourmet cooking—from a friend. As though in anticipation of the impending separation, she had joined a class of about ten other women who took gourmet cooking lessons from one of the outstanding cooks in the area. In the analytic situation, she had referred to this activity in a joking fashion with apparent insight into some of the unconscious roots of her experience. Following termination, she quickly ingratiated herself with her instructor by becoming an excellent student (in her mind, the outstanding student). The relationship became more and more intense and meaningful for her with fantasies similar to those of her past vacations. When the patient sought to accompany him on one of his trips outside the city, the teacher realized the intensity of her involvement, conveyed his alarm, and broke off what he had regarded as a harmless flirtation. This rupture precipitated the intense reaction that prompted the patient to call her analyst.

In retrospect, what had appeared as an effective analytic alliance was functionally a repetition of the fantasy games which the patient had enacted in the early life situation with her mother. Her participation was a matter of compliance with what she viewed as her analyst's expectations. She was the outstanding patient just as she had been the outstanding actress for her mother. The intense relationship she had enacted with the gourmet cook was a displacement from the analytic situation that allowed the patient to endure termination and the post-termination phase. At the presenting level, the enactment of the oedipal fantasy had a crucial self-soothing function as well, as a kind of tension-regulatory device learned from her mother. Fantasying itself constituted a form of the defense transference designed to avoid the reactions she had had to separation from her father and to feeling misunderstood and used by her mother. She had thus introduced into the analytic situation the essence of her early childhood experience. Understanding the meaning of the fantasies was not enough if the states of compliance, the star performances, and the functions of fantasy remained unanalyzed.

As the analytic process was engaged in the second analysis, the nature of the alliance was subjected to care-

ful scrutiny. The compliance which had seemed to sub-
serve a sound working relationship was recognized to be
in the service of fantasy instead. She and her analyst
were engaged in a "shopping spree" through the unconscious; her acquisitions were to exceed by far those of any
of the analyst's other patients. The patient did not easily
accept the analyst's tentative efforts to clarify this state
of affairs. Unlike her ready compliance in reviewing her
fantasies, she now responded to her analyst's interventions as a threat to her basic equilibrium. On the one
hand, there were active and effective ego functions, with
reality processing fairly well developed in confronting
fantasy contents (perhaps in compliance with her analyst). On the other, there was a symbiotic quality to her
fantasying by means of which she experienced the safety
of being with her mother. The function of the analyst was
to explore the original need for and operation of this self-
soothing function. The patient's initial response to the
analyst's interventions was to regard his efforts as a narcissistic assault. As this response was engaged with tact
and understanding, efforts at reconstruction of her infantile situation permitted the development of a significant split in her experience and observations of fantasying.
In the reassuring milieu generated within the analytic
situation, she experienced derivatives of the rage and
depression that she and her mother had warded off in
their fantasies as well as the disillusionment with her
mother for her failure to cope more realistically with her
own feelings or those of her child. The danger in losing
her mother's attention, whatever the cost in constraint
and compliance, became clear to her. The possibility of
a renewed effort at individuation also became apparent.
Problems in the patient's regulation of her self-esteem
were revealed, with it becoming evident that her sense
of defectiveness stemmed from her earliest experiences

with her mother. Being herself carried with it the threat of losing her mother. Shopping sprees, dressing up, fantasies and games restored her sense of well-being. The working through of this pattern in the analysis resulted in a gradual and significant improvement in self-cohesion and self-confidence, the shift from an "as if" alliance to a more substantial joint effort at analytic exploration, and improved self-object differentiation and dyadic reality processing.

This case demonstrates once again the significance for tension regulation of early problems with object relations in a dyadic context. These problems have profoundly disruptive effects on development and are available in derivative form in the analytic process. They are thus subject to clinical intervention and amelioration. In the theoretical section of this monograph, we shall elaborate the theoretical implications of our clinical findings with regard to the analytic alliance, the nature of symptom formation, and the origins and function of the defense transference as a characterological phenomenon.

Chapter 7

Review of the Literature on Follow-Up Studies

Evaluation of the results of analysis has been a recurrent and intriguing concern of analytic writers. It is by no means our purpose here to provide an exhaustive review of every reference to outcome and follow-up. We shall limit our effort to a study of case reports in recent follow-up investigations, and examine the findings in relation to our own thesis.

In 1959, Pfeffer described his procedure for evaluating the results of analysis. We have adopted his method with several revisions. In his follow-up studies, Pfeffer reported several cases demonstrating that residual conflicts were apparent in each instance and were engaged in the follow-up in a kind of mini-analysis that repeated the analytic experience. His reports were directed toward illustrating the repetitive nature of the material and emphasizing that the positive outcome of analysis was the method of coping with conflict learned in the process. To the extent that incompleteness was a factor in the analysis, it was evident in unmodified neurotic conflict without an analytic coping mechanism. Pfeffer's underlying assumption appeared to be that such incompleteness was a function of inadequate resolution of oedipal conflicts.

The first case he reported in 1959 was that of a 23-year-old female music teacher with a homosexual problem. Her analysis proceeded to termination after two years and nine months. The patient gave up her homosexual attachment early in the analysis and experienced a transference neurosis and its resolution. When seen four years after termination, she had married a man with what was perhaps a latent homosexual problem, had had a child with him, and was pregnant again. She reported an "understanding" with her husband which involved a mutual avoidance of digging into each other's past. She knew that her husband had been involved socially with a group of homosexuals in the army. She told of his exaggerated interest in his clothes and that he did not defend her when she complained of his father's kisses and caresses on greeting her. She had suffered a lack of such admiration and attention from her own father, who had had four daughters and who had clearly expressed his preference for boys.

There were other indications of residual conflicts. With regard to her sexual responsiveness, she commented on the fact that she did not have the same thrill when her fiance touched her hand as when her homosexual partner had. She expressed a wish that she could have experienced vaginal orgasms more than the three or four times they had occurred in her marriage. She also described a problem that she had with her two-year-old son, a bright, talkative, active child. He had developed an inordinate love of dolls of a certain kind with rubber fingers that he bit off. Pfeffer was impressed with her discussion of various facets of her son's situation, but he thought that accompanying her tolerance and understanding there had been an encouragement of the child's play with dolls.

In spite of friction in her relationship with her husband, she felt it was a good relationship and expressed a strong love for him. Pfeffer observed that the reconciliation with her parents in the course of the analysis had persisted postanalytically with an ability on her part to discern their good qualities and limitations.

Pfeffer thus noted adaptive improvements in the patient but touched on the evidence of continued conflict in her marriage, her relationship with her in-laws and her decision to discontinue the follow-up after three sessions. The decision was rationalized on reality grounds because of the difficulty in travelling to her appointments in her pregnant state during a busy holiday season.

We would agree that there is evidence of both sustained improvement and continued conflict with regard to neurotic features of the case, but in addition, we would emphasize an aspect of the clinical material related to our own thesis about a developmental outlook. The treating analyst, in his response to Pfeffer's questions, described the analysis as duplicating mainly the relationship with the father with less time devoted to problems about femininity and preoedipal material. In his description of the analytic process there had been a regression from oedipal conflict to an infantile level, with the patient requesting mothering. The management of this development was not elaborated by the treating analyst but he observed that the patient then displayed a reactive "untoward show of independence." We would suggest that derivatives of the show of independence reverberated through her account of postanalytic events, and that it constituted a coping mechanism for the regulation of tension that involved denial, suppression and exaggerated self-reliance. The most dramatic instance was her description of her episode of gastrointestinal bleeding when her child was five months old. She required hospitalization and transfusion; the bleeding recurred once after she left the hospital, with the cause undetermined. There was a marked denial of the serious nature of these two bleeding episodes, which her internist had regarded as life threatening. Her attitude toward illness was a source of tension with her husband, whom she regarded as overconcerned about any illness while she was inclined to minimize it. The "understanding" with her husband not to dig into the past was linked to such a characteristic approach to problems and her decision to terminate the follow-up interviews was reminiscent of that understanding. It is interesting that in the treating analyst's account the untoward show of independence was reactive to her regression and to a need for mothering in the analysis. In our view, problems in separation-individuation were thus engaged revealing pseudo-independence as the defense transference solution to dyadic problems both in tension regulation and in her feminine identification.

The second case Pfeffer reported in 1959 was that of a woman suffering from anxiety, depression, fears of insanity, and concern over increasingly frequent masturbation. Her symptoms had been of three-years duration and had been precipitated by her rejection by a lover, a married man with children. In treatment, the patient was given to unmanageable acting out. She got engaged at the onset of her analysis and threatened marriage throughout the two-year analysis as a form of transference resistance. Post-analytically, she married a self-centered man troubled by premature ejaculation. In the follow-up three years after termination, there was a resurgence of the transference neurosis with fears of knives, angry outbursts at her husband, and a dream that garbage was being dug up in her backyard threatening to undermine the terrain. The case was regarded as one in which the patient's anxiety and depression had been converted to a specific affect—rage—with some development of insight. The follow-up analyst intervened supportively at the end of one session in response to the patient's mounting anger and feelings of being "stirred up." But the basis for these feelings was not elucidated.

Problems in tension regulation and the tolerance and mastery of affects were communicated to the follow-up analyst in her intense transference reactions that seemed unmanageable by the patient and elicited his supportive interventions. Pfeffer notes that this case was his very first follow-up experience and that it was the only case in which open transference reactions were managed by his reassuring responses, in contrast to a spontaneous subsidence of such transferences in the other cases. He implied that if it were not so early in his research, the course of the follow-up might have been different.

Yet the interaction between the patient and the follow-up analyst appears to highlight some of the ingredients in the patient's inability to cope with her rage. Unmanageable acting out as a symptom in the analytic process in itself suggests tension regulatory problems, with recourse to action over introspective problem solving. The acting out was in the form of threatened marriage. The patient reported in the follow-up her anger at her treating analyst for having tried to prevent her from getting married "although she knew why he had done so." She also expressed her suspicions about the fact that her analyst had interrupted her analysis for several months and said that she had never fully accepted the explanation that her analyst had been ill. For her, it remained a personal rejection.

The rage which she had buried readily emerged in the follow-up and the patient's associations suggest some speculations about the outcome of the case. In the follow-up, Pfeffer discerned that her expressed anger at the treating analyst was probably at his attempt to get behind a negative transference to positive feelings; interpreting the anger as a defense against positive oedipal feelings. The patient did resent her treating analyst's effort to ascribe transference significance to her talking about feelings toward her boyfriend. In the follow-up she recalled her parents asking her if she loved them and her father demanding a birthday kiss. As additional perspective, we would suggest that her anger was suppressed by what she perceived as a demand for love. She introduced her garbage dream by saying that in actuality there was a poor family that lived behind her house and the children rummage through the garbage can. The reference to needy children and her knife phobia and fear of violence directed at her own children suggest significant pre-oedipal concerns. We would suggest that the acting out in the analysis of threatened marriage may have been motivated by a wish to find a nurturing, loving relationship and thereby suppress her rage, an affect unacceptable to her parents. In such a context the treating analyst's effort to control her acting out and interpret oedipal conflict would have been experienced by her as a lack of understanding with regard to her dyadic problems. Her defense transference, searching out loving relationships and suppressing her buried rage elicited a benevolent response from the follow-up analyst when he agreed with her that her analysis had certainly been beneficial, agreed that the follow-up interviews were stirring up her feelings and that they could be stopped after a final session in which he could pose a few questions, and reassured her that she had a fear of violent acts rather than really being violent. He also told her in the final session that he knew her treating analyst had really been ill during her analysis and that her unelaborated suspicions were unfounded. The reassurance as a counterdefense transference helped her control and submerge her rage and regain a "good feeling." Her association to the good feeling was the evocation of childhood memories between ages ten and twelve, at home with her mother. When her mother was through with the housework, she and her mother would go shopping and she would have a cozy feeling. The rapprochement based on a suppression and denial of rage is suggestive of a solution to the management of rage rooted in separation-individuation experiences that markedly increased her vulnerability in addressing oedipal conflicts.

In 1961, Pfeffer described the follow-up study of a satisfactory analysis. The patient was a 31-year-old woman who was married to a general practitioner and had two children. She suffered from depersonalization and derealization, experiencing attacks of overwhelming anxiety and paralyzing panic states. Her hands were numb and paralyzed at times and she had the sensation of an entire scene receding from her as she looked at it. She was irritable, screamed at her children in her unsuccessful efforts at discipline, and cried uncontrollably. She was the second of three children. Her father was a businessman of humble origins, her mother self-centered and compulsive. The patient herself was sexually frigid, phobic, with compulsive bathroom behavior, social anxiety, and a writing inhibition. She was diagnosed as a masochistic hysterical character. She had problems with her sense of self and extremely lowered self-esteem.

Pfeffer described four significant themes in her life experience that had been noted by the treating analyst—rejection by her mother, sibling rivalry with her sister, primal scene problems, and the birth of her younger brother. Witnessing the primal scene was regarded as central to her depersonalization. She saw it as a violent assault on a woman who was being murdered or castrated and responded with denial and projection of her own inner excitement. Pfeffer chose to narrow the perspective in his report to derivatives of the primal scene.

Just prior to termination of her seven-year analysis, the patient arranged for a divorce. After termination, she married a passive lawyer, warm and attentive to her needs and unlike her schizoid first husband. In her first marriage, she had managed to close her eyes to her husband's difficulties, and had held herself responsible for his inability to give. Now, after analysis, she was less masochistic and more tolerant of her hostile feelings. Before her analysis, she said, she had been "half dead."

In the follow-up, there was a reactivation of the feelings of the analysis and an upsurge of symptoms during and immediately after the final interview. The depersonalization experience was briefly revisited. According to the treating analyst, the patient was reacting to the knowledge that her sister had gone to see him for a consultation about her child. The treating analyst also noted that the patient had called him to check whether she should discuss with her sister the fact that she could overhear her sister and brother-in-law engaged in sex when she stayed in their guest room. Finally, the patient had had a session with the treating analyst several weeks after the follow-up, in regard to which the treating analyst stated: " . . . this expressed primarily the patient's desire to regain her position with her analyst and to displace the rival, her sister" (p. 715). Pfeffer then went on to say: "Thus, the recurrence of symptoms at the end of the follow-up study primarily, but not altogether, rep-

resents the flare-up of the residual of the childhood pri-
mal-scene experiences" (pp. 715-716).

While it seemed likely to Pfeffer that preoedipal issues
were of some significance in the recurrence of conflicts,
he stated that the material available to him did not permit any judgment about their relative importance. This
might owe, in our view, to Pfeffer's decision to restrict
the material to that involving the primal scene experiences: Such material is easily formulated in oedipal terms
and, indeed, the central focus of the paper is on oedipal
issues. And while we would agree that there are clear
precedents for the patient's concern about overhearing
her sister's sexual relations in her own childhood experiences of the primal scene, and that the conjunction of
this with the patient's jealousy of her analyst's attention
toward her sister suggests a continuing oedipal conflict,
we would also note that this same material can be formulated in different terms: namely, in terms of the patient's problems with her sense of self, precisely those
terms, in fact, in which the treating analyst had formulated the case. Thus, the actual genetic determinants of
this case might rather be the patient's rejection by her
mother and her sibling rivalry with her sister. The treating analyst may have represented the preoedipal mother
for whose attention the patient competed with her sister.

The treating analyst had organized his own account
around the patient's problem with her sense of self. Yet
the central focus in the paper was on oedipal issues and
the treating analyst's judgment was that if there was
unfinished business it was that the positive transference
was not thoroughly analyzed. Pfeffer noted preoedipal
issues as significant but stated that the material available to him did not permit any judgment about its relative
importance. His selective use of the material for his own

significant purpose further reduced the possibility of clarification of earlier developmental determinants of the patient's pathology.

The first case reported in Helene Deutsch's 1959 account of follow-ups on two cases some 25 to 30 years after their analysis illustrates more sharply the problems involved in bringing to follow-up preformed views of the nature and mechanism of the psychoanalytic process. The case described was that of a 20-year-old girl who had attempted suicide as she was about to marry an older man who had left his wife for her. The suicide attempt was understood as stemming from feelings of inferiority early in her life at the time of the birth of her brother, with penis envy prominent. Aggressive jealous reactions had prompted guilt and led to inhibition of her competitive strivings. She repudiated her femininity because it signified a masochistic identification with her mother. Her analysis freed her to marry, to pursue her education as a physicist, and to support her husband when political misfortune interfered with his ability to provide. She had a son late in her marriage who fulfilled her fond hopes for him. The former patient acknowledged that her analyst had helped her very much but stated that analysis itself had given her nothing and that its insights were a hoax, a construction in the mind of the analyst. Deutsch explained the patient's hostile attitude toward analysis as based on narcissistic injury at being confronted with the neurotic past, on the fact that her husband was not favorable to analysis, and on her old hostility and devaluation of her mother, now displaced onto her female analyst. The analysis, according to Deutsch, had permitted the patient to utilize her latent intellectual capacity and achieve a sublimation. She could compete successfully in her professional career and marry the man she had chosen under the influence of the Oedipus complex.

Her emphatic statement that the analysis had given her "nothing" was understood as based on the fact that analysis had not changed the biological fact that she had no penis nor had it healed this "primary narcissistic injury of the phallic past" (p. 454).

Whatever merit such a view may have is limited by the absence of a detailed description by the patient of her own experience. Was her acknowledgment of the "help" she received from her analyst simply in the service of attacking the intellectual content of her analysis, or could she have provided a meaningful account of the emotional significance of the relationship? Were *all* the conclusions of the analysis uniformly regarded as products of the analyst's imagination? A careful investigation might have clarified significant issues in the analytic alliance and their elaboration in her life experience as they rested on earlier developmental problems than the phallic and oedipal determinants of her neurosis. Or at least it might have permitted the formulation of other hypotheses or confirmed Deutsch's view in a more convincing manner. Deutsch does, of course, attribute the success of the analysis to a transformation of the patient's ego in identification with her female analyst and the liberation of her capacity for sublimation, but such conjectures are used to still her own acknowledged doubts and dissatisfaction about her explanations for the patient's analytic experience. The follow-up experience itself is not used as a testing ground for evaluating the nature of the process.

Oremland, Blacker, and Norman (1975) do pursue a research-oriented approach to follow-up in their study of incompleteness in successful analysis. In their method, the follow-up analyst sees the former patient for several interviews to review the analytic experience. Only then does he read the protocol provided by the treating analyst in order to be sure that he has not missed any major issues. They find that the open interviews obtain all the pertinent information.

The first case they described was that of a 26-year-old woman who was suddenly beset by uncontrolled anguish and tears. She was the second of five children. An infant brother had died when she was five and a half. At puberty she had lost another brother, and her mother had had a psychotic break. When her own daughter was six months old she was filled with remorse and tears, quarrelled with her husband, and was unable to be a wife and mother. She achieved sexual pleasure only with fantasies of being tortured. Her analysis, accomplished in three and a half years, dealt with her guilt about her brothers' deaths. In the transference she experienced oedipal feelings about her father, homosexual feelings for her mother, and rivalry with her mother and sister. At termination, there was a resurgence of her symptoms occasioned by the threat of separation with fears of her own death and her analyst's death. Her reactions occasioned a further analysis of early masturbatory and homosexual fantasies.

In the follow-up, she described her husband as critical and perfectionistic. She was guilty about experiencing pleasure when he was so unhappy, a situation, she remarked, reminiscent of her experience with her mother. The problems with her husband were regarded by the researchers as a realistic block to her analysis. Rather than confront them and face the possibility of divorce (and independence), she elaborated a fantasy that her analyst, in a permissive, benevolently omniscient role, had let her "dose" the analytic material according to what she could tolerate. This, according to Oremland et al., was the source of the treatment's "incompleteness." In the year after the follow-up, the patient first sought conjoint treatment for her husband and herself and then returned to her treating analyst for help with issues of separation and divorce.

We would propose an alternative view of the circumstances based on an application of our assessment criteria to the case material. We would stress the deeper aspects of the maternal transference that went unrecognized as a factor in the analytic alliance. In the beginning of the third year of the analysis, there was a shift in the material from oedipal themes to the attachment to the mother. Early masturbatory and homosexual themes were analyzed. In connection with a desire to separate from the analyst, she experienced fears that she would die and that the analyst would die. Fears of death associated with separation were understood as regressions from oedipal conflict. We would regard them further as conflicts rooted in separation-individuation problems. Such conflicts emerge in the termination phase not just as regressive defenses but because the matrix of the analytic process is threatened by the prospect of separation. In this case, triadic conflicts had been resolved to a considerable degree, aggressive competitive feelings were better tolerated, with evidence of a self-analytic function, but dyadic pathology persisted.

In the follow-up, what the patient had "held back" became evident in her account of her highly conflicted relationship with her husband, a relationship reminiscent of that with her mother and characterized by her extreme dependency on him. The disavowed issues of independence and separation from her husband had their roots, in our view, in the dyadic experience with the nurturing mother. Rage and fear of rage in the context of separation-individuation were concealed by masochistic compliance. The threatening analyst's attempt to clarify marital quarrels by investigating their dynamics was vitiated by the manner in which the patient's fantasy structured the analytic situation. Her fantasied relationship with the analyst was the central means by which she regulated tension. It evidenced a problem in object relations presumably based on very early developmental experience. Indeed, her transference fantasy suggested that her view of reality was compromised by the need to preserve a nurturing dependent relationship. She disavowed and denied the intolerable possibility of separation from her husband and experienced that very disavowal and denial as a benign regulation of tension by her analyst, thereby preserving her relationship with *him*. Such disavowal and denial in her relationship with her mother may be inferred from the childhood background of sibling death and the maternal potential for psychosis, actualized in the patient's adolescence. Self-soothing was thus at the expense of reality testing, just as it must have been in her early childhood, particularly in the management of rage associated with separation. The follow-up process did help the patient understand the unresolved problems with separation in her life, and she returned for further analysis for help with the issues of separation and divorce.

The second case described by Oremland et al. was that of Mr. H., a 32-year-old salesman with marital and work problems and conflicts with his parents. He was the only child of an accountant and a schoolteacher. He described his father as passive and preoccupied and his mother as intrusive and aggressive. At the age of two, he was hospitalized for a severe illness. He was alone a great deal as a child because his mother worked. He explored her things, tasted and ate strange items. He developed mechanical and mathematical skills. Later, his relationships were limited by his demandingness and "stupidity."

He was nicknamed "Zero" by his friends. He married shortly after graduating from the university and immediately was involved in constant fighting with his wife.

In his analysis he demonstrated restlessness and wild posturing on the couch in the first months as a reaction against passivity and immobility. He had an early dream of free association in front of his analyst while lying on the floor of the kitchen in his own home. The dream was a reliable indication of his intense desire to have an intimate association with his analyst but in a submissive role, as a child. At work he acted out a caricature of the supersalesman, as though he could control everybody by being the most valuable employee. He was fired as unmanageable. His exhibitionistic impulses were apparent in the analysis in impulses to urinate and to compete with his passive father. He also experienced wishes to be "aimed" by mother and regarded his ability to take initiative as losing mother. He had a confusion about right and left, front and back, and in relation to disturbed body imagery elaborated memories of adolescent voyeuristic and transvestite behavior. He described intense homosexual fears related to his difficulty in learning from men. He cruised black areas to tease prostitutes on his way to the analyst's office as an exaggerated version of his early adolescent behavior. Wishes for a "real" relationship with his analyst emerged in which he was the equal, in total control, or completely dependent. Their transference origins were clarified. The cruising behavior was understood as his effort to be in contact with his mother and yet express his independence. The pursuit of debased women ceased and competitive conflicts were analyzed. With general improvement, a termination date was discussed. As the date approached he fell again into inactivity with magical expectations of being saved. The interpretation of the wishes involved permitted a successful conclusion of the analysis five and a half years after it was begun.

In the follow-up, the former analysand presented a kind of obtuseness similar to his behavior in the analysis, expressing his need to be cared for, even though his accomplishments had been sustained and he had learned a great deal about himself. The symptom of cruising in the black community had returned post-analytically. The research team felt that Mr. H. had suppressed the activity in his analysis in order to preserve its transference context. He carried a notebook for his thoughts and dreams (as a representation of his continued communication with his analyst) and kept it always in his possession. In the view of the researchers, the need to live out the transference had not been fully analyzed. He returned to his treating analyst a year after the follow-up for face-to-face psychotherapy. His view of the termination of his analysis was that his analyst had been building him up like his mother had. He treasured an actual social encounter with his analyst in the course of his analysis and had resisted efforts to analyze its significance.

The nature of the incompleteness in this case was understood to be based on resistance on the part of the patient to analysis of the transference, thereby to secure the illusion of a "real" relationship with the analyst. It suggests once again the importance of object relations in the analytic experience. Obtuseness had been a persisting mode of engaging parental care. To the extent that it failed to engage the analyst adaptively, a fantasied "real" relationship was evoked as a substitute, a solution that must have corresponded to what the patient had done as a deprived child in the absence of his mother. The patient's characterological defense was maintained unaltered by the analysis of later neurotic conflicts. In our view, it reflected earlier developmental concerns involving the nature of the rapprochement experience with the mother and the accompanying development of reality processing. The incompleteness of the analytic effort could therefore involve not simply a resistance on the part of the patient but a misguided focus on the part of the analyst at termination. The wish to be "taken care of" as a basis for resurgent symptomatology at termination may be interpreted as "defensive" behavior, without adequate regard for the origins of the defense in pre-neurotic symptomatology.

Norman, Blacker, Oremland, and Barrett, in a third case studied by the same group, reviewed the analysis of Dr. Smith, himself an analyst. They described the revival of the analytic process in the follow-up, and the emergence of positive and negative transference residuals of oedipal conflicts and their resolution. An undercurrent in the account was Dr. Smith's concern about perfection, whether his analysis had been a great analysis or a worthless analysis. In a sense, it was as though his analytic experience had been a performance for his analyst. The mobilization of narcissistic core reactions with his mother was suggested by the account as a characterological mold for his responses in the analysis and the follow-up, and a focus for his anxiety. The authors concentrated on the transference neurosis and the development of a self-analytic capacity in this case of a satisfactory analysis. But while their interest was not in incompleteness, the narcissistic problem might well have represented an area of unfinished business, suggesting earlier developmental issues worthy of analysis.

Firestein (1978), in his book *Termination in Psychoanalysis*, studied, by means of limited follow-ups, a number of cases from the point at which they appeared headed for termination. In the termination phase he recorded interviews with the treating analysts (candidates) at intervals of some weeks and reviewed summaries of the pre-termination analyses. He gathered metapsychological statements of the analyses from the treating analysts. When possible he met with the patients for an interview a year or more after termination. He also consulted the faculty supervisors active on the cases. This wealth of information was reduced in the book, however, to condensed and selective accounts of the cases. Firestein's conclusions have an almost phenomenological flavor to them, in the way they identify themes, affects, and kinds of reactions associated with termination. The brevity of the follow-ups permitted only subjective and impressionistic accounts of the patients' reactions to their analytic experiences and provide little evidence on which to base an independent judgment of the nature of the process, what was accomplished and what was left incomplete. The study emphasized the need for consistent criteria of evaluation and a systematic approach to reviewing protocols of the analytic experience and its follow-up.

The importance of analytic depth in follow-up studies, at least for the purpose of formulating hypotheses and testing them, is illustrated by our own experience with the two cases reported in Chapters 2 and 3, in which ongoing second analyses provided significant information for the follow-up on the follow-up. The findings confirmed our impressions of the importance of early developmental determinants in the analytic process.

Our review of the literature on follow-up studies emphasizes the potential for ongoing useful research on the nature of the analytic process and the central determinants for change. Incompleteness and development are the essence of any living process. Repetition of the analytic experience in conflict and in solution allows for renewed efforts at explanation of success and failure. New observations and new perspectives may emerge to improve the explanatory power of psychoanalytic theory. The hypotheses that evolve in such research require continued careful examination and testing. As a step in pursuit of that goal, we have found that our hypotheses could be usefully applied in reformulating the clinical experiences reported in follow-up studies in the literature. It is our hope that this may promote an ongoing research dialogue toward the further elucidation of questions and hypotheses about the outcome of psychoanalytic treatment.

Part II

Theoretical Implications

Chapter 8

Discussion of the Fate of the Analytic Alliance

The clinical studies of the analytic process reported in Part I permit us to set forth the following conclusions:

1. Analysis of the transference neurosis reveals repetitive patterns of conflict as a response to stress and that these patterns persist post-analytically. The pace of their repetition increases as the analysis progresses and as the patient's ego is sensitized to manifestations of conflict. The effect of analysis is not the obliteration of conflict but a change in the potential for coping with conflict, evident in a greater tolerance for and improved mastery of frustration, anxiety, and depression. After termination, these coping mechanisms operate chiefly in the form of a preconscious self-analytic function, in identification with the analyst's effort to observe, understand, and integrate psychic phenomena.

2. The analytic alliance serves as a matrix for the development of the transference neurosis and its re-solution, engaging at the deepest level the basic transference potential of the analysand. Early narcissistic and

dyadic developmental problems may be silently imbricated in the analytic relationship. Our experience in follow-up studies has persuaded us of the relative disregard of the significance of such early developmental determinants in the analytic process. The adaptive solutions of the separation-individuation experience of the patient form an integral part of the alliance. Dyadic and symbiotic defects become particularly apparent around separations and efforts at mastery of new skills, as in the termination phase of an analysis. They require appropriate analytic interventions beyond their interpretation as regressive defenses.

3. Our case illustrations demonstrate as well the need for attention to early developmental determinants of the analysand's tension-regulatory mechanisms as these present themselves symptomatically in the analytic process. They include modes of behavior which antedate psychoneurotic phenomena and contribute to them. States of overstimulation, frantic efforts at their solution, and other patterns of response to these states may seriously limit the effectiveness of interpretations directed at structural conflicts.

4. Characterological traits and defenses develop as an adaptive solution to separation-individuation problems and then serve as a defense against oedipal conflicts. Their genetic roots require analytic exploration for effective re-solution of psychoneurotic conflicts.

In the last three chapters, we shall explore the implications of our findings about early developmental determinants in the analytic process, considering their role in the analytic alliance, in tension-regulatory aspects of symptom formation, and in character development.

THEORETICAL ORIENTATION

The analytic process engages in derivative form the entire developmental history of the individual. In the transference neurosis, there is a repetition of the neurotic conflicts of the structured personality. In the analytic alliance, earlier developmental elements are imbricated. Our case illustrations, through a focus on the fate of the analytic alliance, demonstrate the need for analytic attention to earlier layers of childhood experience, intimately associated with the phenomena of separation-individuation. We have found it useful conceptually to divide the alliance into two parts on a developmental axis. The first is a matrix which reflects the vicissitudes of dyadic experiences and the quality of the resources acquired as a consequence of them: self constancy, object constancy, and a self-soothing regulatory function. In our criteria for assessment, ego functions such as basic trust, dyadic relations and dyadic reality processing, and the tolerance for anxiety, depression, and frustration are included in the matrix. In our view, the matrix is an aspect of the alliance associated with such concepts as Freud's "basic transference" and Gitelson's "diatrophic function of the analyst." As a focus of analytic interest, it confronts the analyst with formative stages of elementary psychic structure and defects in structure. The second aspect of the analytic alliance to which we refer is the collaborative and analytic effort, based on later developmental accretions as well as earlier ones, and, classically, concerned with the management of intrapsychic conflicts. It is related to Greenson's "working alliance," and has its outcome in the development of a self-analytic function. In the widened scope of psychoanalytic practice, the collaborative effort is directed not only to the resolution of intersystemic conflicts but to the recognition and modification of earlier developmental structural deficits and distortions in tension-regulatory functions in the matrix of the alliance.

Settlage (in Winestein, 1973) characterized human psychological development as a lifelong process of separation-individuation in a panel discussion on that topic based on Mahler's work. He described a progression from rudiments of psychic structure through libidinal object constancy to increasing separation from the original love objects with correlated internalizations and rearrangements of self- and object representations and a hierarchical development of psychic regulatory structure and functions. Separation-individuation is revisited and reworked in each successive stage of development with a steadily reduced dependence on the external parental object. The distinction between normative regression in the service of the ego and pathological regression rests on the degree of success or failure in infantile separation-individuation, in particular, on the extent to which the mother-child relationship is internalized. As Speers (in Winestein, 1973) observed, consolidation of libidinal object constancy occurs through recapitulation of early stages in the face of threats of actual separation from the love object, with further stabilization of internal images.

Kohut (1971) has described the parallel development of a cohesive self, which might be viewed as a kind of self constancy analogous to object constancy. In the process of internalization, the child acquires a self-soothing and self-caring function in identification with the mother's ministrations. The complex function that results attests to the nature and effectiveness of the solution of separation-individuation anxieties about merger and separateness, love and aggression, and expectations of self and objects. Assessment of the self-soothing function includes a review of capacities for self- and object differentiation, self and object constancy, dyadic relationship, dyadic reality processing, and the resulting inner resources and methods of coping with frustration and anxiety.

In the same panel, Settlage emphasized the repetitive themes apparent in development. The separation anxiety of the practicing subphase, with the child's need for the physical proximity of the mother for emotional refueling, is repeated in the rapprochement subphase with its pressing desire for the mother to share every new acquisition of skill and experience. It is represented once again in oedipal-stage castration anxiety with its conflict over relinquishment of the parent as a sexual object. The road to mastery from object constancy through development of a self-soothing function through internalization of parental controls in the superego reduces the fear of loss and separation. Yet in latency separation anxiety and fears of death are occasioned once again by ambivalence and guilt as neurotic conflicts unfold between the drives and the newly internalized regulatory functions.

Mahler (1972a) explained the "low-keyedness" in infants experiencing temporary separation from their mothers during the practicing subphase as part of an effort to maintain an intrapsychic union with the symbiotic partner, an ideal state of self. The lost narcissism of childhood, gathered from ideal self concepts and idealized love objects and selfobjects, finds expression in the ego ideal, formed in response to normative psychic traumata of separation. In adolescence, the ego with its expanded resources confronts the task of relinquishing the ties to internalized infantile love objects and selfobjects. Citing the work of Blos (1967), Settlage designated the consequences of this adolescent effort as a kind of "secondary object constancy." In a parallel manner, with the modifications in ego ideal and superego, secondary self constancy is attained through a reorganization of the self.

Separation is central to internalization and identification at every level of experience, and the nature of the separation influences the internal consequences of the encounter. In the simplest terms, conflict-ridden or unempathic separation may be experienced as rejection, mobilizing destructive rage, impairing positive identification, and heightening the influence of harsh or sadistic regulatory controls. Zetzel (1965b) has suggested that, in instances of traumatic early experiences involving separation, the crucial question is whether the patient can achieve a real separation by internalizing the relationship with the analyst through identification and object representation. The patient must have the capacity to tolerate and master depressive affect and regressive forms of anxiety that may emerge in the face of threatened loss. In extreme cases of traumatic early experiences involving separation, Zetzel has noted that the continued availability of the analyst is an indispensable prerequisite for the maintenance of more mature ego functions. Loewald (1962) has described extreme cases in which the existence and/or the loss of the object may be denied. Instead of internalization of the relationship for the provision of stability, external substitutions may be sought, as, for example, clinging to relatives and friends, with a loss of the ability to form new relationships or stable sublimations. These extreme reactions suggest the likelihood of pathological outcomes for the alliance.

Fleming (1972), in her paper on early object deprivation and transference in parent-loss cases, set forth the thesis that object deprivation in childhood results in inadequate internalization of early symbiotic experiences that provide the emotional wherewithal for later ego development. Such patients attempt to restore and maintain a sense of the presence of the needed object in fantasy and suffer an arrest in ego development, a distortion in reality processing, and a problem in establishing a working alliance. The parent-loss patient requires "empathically symbiotic" responses from the analyst that establish an appropriate matrix for the interruption of transference defenses against grief and mourning, permitting the establishment of a collaborative alliance and the resumption of ego development.

In neurotic character formation, while there may be no abrupt and permanent loss, unempathic mothering or relative unavailability at critical periods may occur for a variety of reasons. Such experiences leave their mark in less than ideal matrices for the alliance.

THE TREATMENT SITUATION

The gratifications inherent in the analytic situation may themselves enable an analytic process to unfold and yet also serve as a defensive shield, ego syntonic to patient and analyst alike, against the recognition of defects in the alliance on a dyadic level. These might contribute to what Gero (Hurn, 1973) has described as a possible post-analytic problem, "a repressed bad parent transference." One possible source of this might be that the contributions of gratifying elements of the alliance to the "analytic cure" may be too reminiscent of the beneficial effects of hypnosis and suggestion for the comfort of the analyst who prefers to think he functions by interpretation of structural conflict alone. Conversely, prepared by his theory for a period of good feeling and honest mutual regard as the transference neurosis is resolved and transference distortions are stripped away, the analyst may find that the recrudescence of infantile longings and rage and the phenomenology of separation-individuation pose particularly poignant problems.

The developmentally early origin of the gratifying aspect of the alliance is suggested by the description of it post-analytically as a "friendly spirit" or "a benevolent presence," language that seems consonant with Schafer's (1968) concept of primary-process presences. In our view, the benign presence represents an internalization of the function of the analyst as a regulator of tension. States of overstimulation and boredom, frantic efforts at their solution, and attitudes of compliance and overidealization may seriously limit the effectiveness of interpretive efforts prematurely focused on structural conflicts. They pose problems in the alliance requiring analytic activity directed toward the establishment and maintenance of a "holding environment" and the correction of defects in structure.

The analyst may function in this area in a psychoterapeutic fashion, availing himself of intrinsic supportive features of the analytic situation: the regularity and frequency of visits, an analytic stance with careful attention to the patient's productions, the exercise of tact, appropriate dosage of analytic interventions, and an appreciation of the mirroring and idealizing aspects of the transference. In this regard, Dewald (1976) has emphasized the importance of the real behavior of the analyst in maintaining an analytic posture in the face of regressive transference experiences of the patient. Based on the nature of the analytic experience the internalization of the analyst as a regulator of tension may then be as a selfobject, as a benign presence, as remembered qualities of the analyst, or by identification with the analyst's empathic understanding as part of the self. Such an outcome, to the extent that it deals with early developmental defects, may be regarded as a psychotherapeutic accretion that fills in for an early deprivation or serves as a patch on early traumata.

A more analytic approach would involve transmuting internalizations as described by Kohut. These occur as a result of the working through of separations and failures in empathy and the consequent identification of problems in the alliance, with the eventual discovery, reconstruction, and interpretation of their genetic roots from the patient's behavior and productions. Transmuting internalizations tend toward the development of a self-soothing function and greater self and object constancy with less reliance on external objects to substitute post-analytically for the nurturing empathic function of the analyst. Such changes would facilitate the appropriate integration of motives and ego resources as part of the organization of the self rather than in the service of appeasement of hostile introjects.

Kohut, in exploring the earliest developmental experiences of his patients, focused on the vicissitudes of narcissism, increasingly eschewing conflict psychology in explaining the consequences of failures in empathy on the consolidation of a cohesive self and the internalization of an ego ideal. Inadequate empathy leads to narcissistic rage. Drive derivatives are present as fragmentation products. Efforts to confront and tame the drives are unfounded and misguided in his view. The child's ineffectual rage results from the loss of hope of fulfillment of its goals, and the analytic situation provides an empathic grasp of the patient's dilemma and its reconstruction and resolution by transmuting internalization. Kernberg, insisting that he treats the same range of psychopathology, has maintained that it is necessary to pursue conflicts with instinctual tensions as the central issue. It is his contention that the analyst's deliberate assumption of an empathic stance distorts and submerges the basis for the patient's anger. Such ideological differences become operative in formulations and interventions and presumably in analytic outcomes. In that regard, they offer a fertile field for follow-up studies exploring early developmental features of the analytic process.

Kohut has noted that in narcissistic personality disorders "narcissistic transferences are the therapeutic activities of developmental phases which probably correspond predominantly to the transitional period between a late part of the stage of symbiosis and an early part of the stages of individuation in Mahler's sense" (1971, p. 220). His observations were made in a clinical intrapsychic frame of reference. His theoretical view was of a narcissistic line of development of object libidinal ties. Modell (1976) has suggested that in the narcissistic personality disorders the center of action is the provision of a setting and mutative interpretations to facilitate ego consolidation and a therapeutic alliance with the eventual emergence of a transference neurosis. By contrast, he described the holding environment of the analytic situation in the transference neurosis as functioning like a vessel or container and providing "the necessary background of safety to support illusions" (p. 305).

A relevant question may be raised as to whether or not it is a fallacy to reduce problems with object loss and separation conflicts in patients who have achieved self and object constancy to separation-individuation problems that antedate the development of such constancy. In this regard, it seems to us no more a fallacy to recognize and investigate derivatives of the earliest psychological phenomena in the analytic alliance than it has been a fallacy to attend to derivatives of oral and anal libidinal and aggressive phenomena in patients who have achieved a resolution of the Oedipus complex and acquired a superego and ego ideal. It would be naïve to suggest that any phenomena in the psychoanalytic situation precisely recapitulate infantile and childhood experience. Analysts always work with derivatives and complex formations. The structure of the container should not be taken for granted and may even be improved by analytic effort directed toward its most archaic precursors.

A developmental view of the relationship between narcissistic and object libidinal phenomena in early childhood is certainly open to continuing scrutiny. Modell emphasized object libidinal ties in the "holding environment." He found recapitulated within it the broader caretaking functions of the parent in relation to the child, the provision of an illusion of safety and protection. In the narcissistic frame of reference, Kohut would presumably have regarded such features as the functions of a selfobject.

From another research perspective, the child observations of Mahler, theoretically directed toward object constancy rather than the cohesive self, provide a conceptual framework that may be usefully placed in relation to the approach to narcissistic problems. The translation of a behavioral observational mode to an intrapsychic investigation poses serious problems and yet seems feasible. The observations themselves are psychoanalytically informed and permit a bridge to intrapsychic comprehensibility through the formulation of hypotheses about phenomena in the analytic process that may then be studied with the usual analytic tools. A diagnostic formulation with regard to the configuration of the rapprochement phase may well prove to be a useful orientation to an analytic case as the necessary clinical information becomes available. As a developmental vantage point, it affords the observer a significant view of an individual growth process. If the analyst is prepared to observe the relevant data, derivatives may be analyzed

as isolated transferences or in their possibly phasic repetitions. It is a conceptual approach that deserves analytic exploration, supplying a new metaphor for the
analytic process.

The concept of the rapprochement subphase appears
to be particularly promising as an avenue for the apprehension and understanding of separation phenomena in
the analytic process and particularly in the termination
phase of an analysis. Mahler, Pine, and Bergman (1975)
have described the rapprochement subphase as an important crossroad in personality development. In their
view, the rapprochement crisis may become and remain
an unresolved intrapsychic conflict, an unfavorable point
of fixation in ego development and object relations which
interferes with oedipal development and resolution. It is
our hypothesis that the parent-child relationship in the
rapprochement phase may be paradigmatic, leaving its
mark in an enduring pattern on the whole area of the
acquisition of independent ego functions and determining
the degree to which they are subject to involvement in
conflict. Ideally, parental empathy balances the child's
need for support and his capacity for independent function so as to maintain optimal frustration and permit
individuation, with the development of object constancy,
self constancy, and a tolerable ego ideal. Every growth
point with its accompanying separation provides a renewed test of the resources stemming from progressive
neutralization and of the special vulnerability introduced
by early dyadic and symbiotic defects. The termination
phase represents such a growth point, calling upon the
analysand to consolidate the ego resources developed in
the course of his analysis in an independently operative
preconscious self-analytic function. As we have previously emphasized, the consolidation of this function appears to rest on an identification with the analyzing

function of the analyst as an outcome of mourning the loss of the analyst. The establishment and maintenance of conditions which enhance the development and utilization of such a function require the attention of the analyst throughout the analysis but particularly in the termination phase.

Specific patterns of child-parent interaction with regard to expectations about separation and individuation appear to be particularly significant at termination. In any analysis, of course, they are a matter of interest with regard to tolerance of incomplete growth or variable rates of growth in ego functions or solutions to particular conflicts. In derivative form, unrealistic expectations of the analyst, albeit unverbalized in an explicit fashion, constitute an unfortunate iatrogenic factor affecting the self-regulatory system. If cyclic repetitions of conflict in response to stress are viewed simply as resistance, and if the obliteration of conflict is seen as the analytic goal, unrealistic expectations follow, affecting the further development of the patient. At an opposite extreme, the analyst who believes that only candidates and rare patients develop the wherewithal for self-analytic progress may communicate his view by interpreting for the patient at a point in the process when the patient may be prepared to perform the task himself. If the analytic goal were the facilitation of the development of a self-analytic function as a form of individuation, the analyst would be alert to residual problems interfering with such a function, particularly residual transferences of the rapprochement phase activated by the prospect of termination.

An interpretive effort directed at such residual transferences would represent a proper regard, in our view, for derivatives of separation-individuation as they inevitably emerge at the end of the process. The problem of mourning as an issue in the termination phase must, of course, in a crucial sense remain preparatory. Only when regular meetings are discontinued can the full range of reactions be mobilized and the state of the defenses and ego resources tested. A focus on the issues of separation-individuation in their developmental (transference) context would provide a suitable frame of reference for mourning in the termination phase and for the post-analytic experience as well.

Chapter 9

Symptom Formation in a
Developmental Context

In his elucidation of the paradigm of psychoneurotic symptom formation in the *Introductory Lectures* (1916-1917), Freud noted, in a philosophical aside, that "in scientific matters, people are very fond of selecting one portion of the truth, putting it in place of the whole, and then disputing the rest, which is no less true, in favor of this one position" (p. 346). In fact, he attributed the rise of divergent schools of opinion in the psychoanalytic movement to such a process. At the time, he was considering such controversies as the significance of the ego instincts versus the sexual instincts, constitutional factors as against traumatic, and real current tasks versus past experience. He essentially adopted an operational view of the problem of controversy, suggesting that interest in the motives of men should be subordinated to what they actually do in considering their contributions. The ideal of scientific inquiry had a pragmatic importance. Freud's self-critical methodological commentary, prompted by such an ideal and so regularly present in his works, is no less evident in the pages of his lectures. Its

181

relevance will be highlighted as we elaborate his schema, as a means of establishing and clarifying an overriding developmental focus on symptom formation. The task is simplified by the fact that a developmental approach was central to Freud's own thinking. Parenthetically, such an approach holds promise for a scientific integration of some aspects of divergent schools of analytic thought.

The paradigm of psychoneurotic symptom formation proposed by Freud in the *Introductory Lectures* may be briefly stated. It was based on the topographic model and the precursors of the structural model, and its basic outline remained essentially unchanged in its further elaboration by Freud. An external frustration in love or of competitive strivings in adult life precipitated a manifest regression or introversion, in which the gratifying play of fantasy was drawn into service as a healing force. Daydreaming, for example, constituted a flexible and refreshing retreat that permitted a subsequent return to the rigors of reality with replenished resources. In persons with serious libidinal fixations, however, a further regression occurred. Unconscious positions of libidinal fixation were cathected, reviving old libidinal object attachments in an effort to recapture an earlier level of experience and gratification. Impulses in infantile form as related to their infantile objects pressed for expression and were confronted by the weakened defensive resources of preconscious functioning. The increase in undischarged object libido manifested itself in anxiety and threatened to produce an "actual neurosis." At this point, the initial external frustration had been replaced by an internal frustration. Freud regarded this traumatic state of affairs as a current version of the "actual neurotic core" of a psychoneurosis. In the final step of compromise formation, the psychoneurotic symptoms were formed as an attempt at solution that avoided continued exposure to a traumatic state. The symptoms were a behavioral resultant of conflicting forces, drives, and controls, affording some degree of expression to infantile wishes at the expense of ego mastery. They constituted a foreign body in the ego that had to be rationalized.

In Freud's view, this entire process of adult symptom formation had its precursors in childhood at the time of the resolution of the Oedipus complex. Undischarged libido directed at incestuous objects then threatened the child with an actual neurosis in a specific genetic context. Developmentally, as the internalization of the superego proceeded, there were transient psychoneurotic symptoms of the infantile neurosis. With the strengthening of appropriate character defenses and controls, the ego gained ascendancy and the symptoms subsided. The earlier experience then served as a model for later derivative symptom formations under conditions of frustration. The vulnerability and capacity for compromise formation thus had a longitudinal history.

In his discussion of external frustration, Freud noted that there were various solutions possible other than psychoneurotic symptom formation. People might endure frustration or find suitable substitute gratifications. The plasticity of the sexual instinct permitted partial instinct gratification to substitute for the whole and a wide range of changes in object was possible. There were also sublimatory solutions. Why then did patients fall ill? He focused on developmental inhibition as a solution to the puzzle, by which he meant a libidinal fixation. In advancing his explanations, he questioned the activity of the ego in the origin of symptoms, but remained intent on defending libidinal explanations against assault. Critics of analysis might regard the ego as consciously active at every point and take the "ego's counterfeit as sterling coin." He cited Adler as an example of a critic who regarded the neurotic character as a cause of the neurosis rather than its consequence. He questioned how to do justice to the part played by the ego in symptom formation without grossly neglecting the findings of analysis, predicting that eventually it would be done. In a prescient survey of the developmental scene, he pointed to the investigation of the narcissistic neurosis as an endeavor that would permit a proper assessment of the share taken by the ego in the onset of the neuroses.

Reviewing his own approach, Freud questioned why he did not start an explanation of symptom formation with the common neurotic state. Was it because he was intent on demonstrating the importance of the libidinal factor in symptom formation? He denied this, emphasizing that the actual neurosis was itself in his experience a confirmation of the libido theory, since the anxiety symptoms were the result of a marked increase in undischarged libido—the significance of the sexual life sprang to the eye. In discounting the significance of the actual neurotic state, he stated that he was rather motivated by the fact that the anxiety was without psychological meaning.

In "Types of Onset of Neurosis" (1912), Freud emphasized that actual neurotic symptoms could not be analyzed. Symptoms such as constipation, headaches, fatigue, sleeplessness, and bodily preoccupations, when subsumed under such categories as anxiety neurosis, neurasthenia, and hypochondriasis, could not be traced back historically or symbolically. They were not the product of conflict between intrapsychic agencies and could not be understood as substitutes for sexual gratification. They were current noxae, signs that the ego was overwhelmed by a quantity of libido. He granted that analytic treatment might make actual neurotic symptoms more tolerable or enable escapes by change in sexual regime. Acknowledging the possibility of error over the theoretical problem of the actual neurosis, his anticipated consolation was that it would involve an advance in knowledge. In the *Introductory Lectures,* actual neurotic symptoms were ascribed to a somatic cause, in keeping with the idea that they might represent a transformation of dammed-up libido into toxic products that had a chemical explanation. They were outside the realm of analysis. Libidinal excitations were identified as like the grain of sand in the oyster, an irritant around which the pearl takes form. Psychoneurotic symptoms were thus given a place of honor and actual neurotic symptoms dismissed as somatic irritants.

In *Inhibitions, Symptoms and Anxiety* (1926), there was an attempt to bring the actual neurosis back into psychoanalysis with a unified anxiety theory (Sadow, Gedo, Miller, Pollock, Sabshin and Schlessinger, 1968). A traumatic situation was defined as an experience of helplessness, relative to the strength of the ego. In the *New Introductory Lectures* (1933), Freud explicitly rejected his previous view that anxiety in the actual neurosis was transformed libido. Actual neurotic anxiety was perceived as a basic biological response to threat and the actual neurosis was retained at the core of the transference neurosis. Although that suggests a central position, the dictum that the actual neurosis was not subject to analytic investigation, and that analytic influence over it could only be indirect, limited the potential for discovery, and for the elaboration of theory and technique with regard to actual neurotic phenomena as they became evident in the analytic situation. The technical prescription was for a careful study and interpretation of intrapsychic conflicts. The psychic energy freed by the resolution of intrapsychic conflict would then enable the adult to exercise his more mature resources to find a better adaptation in life. The criteria for analysis incorporated this view of the process, in the sense that to be suitable for analysis the analysand was assumed to have traversed earlier developmental stages in reasonably good fashion and to have acquired the necessary ego resources.

Greenacre (1971) has pointed out that "most of Freud's publications deal with this very early period as though the disturbances were incorporated into the constitution, which might then be more or less generally pathogenic." The subsequent history of psychoanalysis would seem to have provided sufficient experience and information for considerable reformulation and change of our view of the analytic process. Yet Greenacre in her review of the effects of developments in ego psychology on psychoanalysis stressed the lag in the application of analytic insights and their assimilation in practice. She described the fact that her own initial contributions to psychoanalysis were at first set aside as speculative and non-analytic, only later to be referred to as classics. Efforts to find a place in adult analysis for clinical findings from preverbal stages of infancy, the observation of children, and the efforts at analysis of a variety of character problems continue to meet considerable resistance. The questions raised in the forties continue to be raised in the eighties. What relevance is there in the experience of separation-individuation for adult analysis? If a patient has once achieved self and object constancy, how can the factors significant in its origins and maintenance play any part in later separations in an analysis? Can the nonverbal experiences of individuation be repeated and observed in an analytic context? Is this not an imaginative exercise of the analyst, a personal mythology, a theoretical and technical aberration?

The analytic literature is replete with case examples in which the study of the ego and its defenses and adaptations have been elaborated. The tendency is to regard them as special cases and as special problems with regard to technique. The emphasis is often on serious pathology, borderline states and severe ego distortions. The case reports are often sensitively drawn and demonstrate hard-won insights into the inner workings of individual patients. Yet the emphasis on unique qualities and deep pathology in special cases maintains an unfortunate focus on symptom *formation* that hardens conventional wisdom and knowledge.

Zetzel presented an interesting view of her own psychoanalytic experience in 1964. Her training had combined academic psychiatry at Maudsley and psychoanalysis at the London Institute. She was alerted early to the limitations of instinctual fixation as an exclusive basis for diagnostic evaluation. Aware of its limitations, she described how disconcerted she was by premature efforts to apply the theory and findings of psychoanalysis as then constituted to the entire range of her patients. At the Boston Institute of Psychoanalysis in 1950, she found herself playing devil's advocate, emphasizing the essentials of formal psychiatric evaluation to counteract naïve applications of libido theory and the structural model. In her work she came to emphasize a developmental approach to analysis, citing the crucial importance of object relations at all periods of life and of their origin in the early mother-child relationship as a continuing determinant of definitive psychic structure and function.

The critical theoretical shift in orientation indeed involves a developmental approach, in which the patient's experiences and symptoms are explored in the psychoanalytic situation in the context of the whole of childhood and not limited to the explanatory concepts of the structural model. For the structural model tends to limit the view to the situation prevailing after the resolution of the Oedipus complex. Pregenital factors, in our view, should not simply be incorporated as regressive phenomena in the configuration of oedipal conflict. Character studies should not be special cases. In every analytic case, the full range of developmental experience deserves attention. Ego fixations and tension regulation are worthy objects of investigation in their own right and specific patterns of individuation may crucially affect the outcome of any analytic process.

In the effort to integrate early and late theorizing about symptomatology, the concept of actual neurotic anxiety appears to be a key to the dilemma. It is our thesis that the fate of actual neurotic anxiety as a theoretical concept was a central factor inhibiting the development of psychoanalytic theory and technique, whether its place in symptom formation was repeated as dogma or whether the concept itself was cursorily dismissed as obsolete. Common neurotic anxiety, the core of the psychoneurosis, must be fully reclaimed as a proper focus of analytic interest. Gedo and Goldberg (1973) have suggested that a series of models are necessary to explain clinical phenomena in their full breadth and depth. Dorpat (1976) reiterates their analysis of the problem. He emphasizes that psychic conflict prior to the differentiation of tripartite structure occurs in the area of object relations and cites clinical evidence against the universal applicability of structural explanations of depression and hysteria.

Viewed in a developmental context, the significance of actual neurotic anxiety is not lessened by the fact that it lacks symbolic meaning. As a symptom, it demonstrates that the level of stimulation exceeds the capacity of the organism for mastery. It constitutes a dramatic distress signal, throughout development and in the analytic process as well. As an ingredient in psychoneurotic symptom formation, it makes its presence known from the very onset of the adult neurosis in that it is the individual's response to an external frustration that disrupts an existing adaptation and tests his resources to tolerate and master frustration in an intrapsychic context. Psychoneurotic symptomatology is a defense against experiencing the actual neurotic state. The logical consequence of this view is that as psychoneurotic symptomatology is stripped away, actual neurotic problems (i.e., inadequacies in structure created by earlier developmental vicissitudes) will become apparent. Such structural deficits are evidenced throughout the analytic process, particularly in reaction to separations but also in response to a variety of stresses, including the demands of the analytic situation itself. To some extent they are subject to the beneficial effects of being "worked through" in the benign presence and with the empathic guidance of the analyst, with accretions in the capacity for reality processing and in a variety of ego functions. The distress signals would, of course, vary widely in their frequency and intensity from patient to patient, depending on many variables, but it is interesting to note that in a well-defended neurotic for whom psychoneurotic symptom formation has been a relatively successful adaptation, actual neurotic anxiety may become more evident in the termination phase, when the issues of separation-individuation are most dramatically engaged for every patient.

What then are we to regard as symptoms and conflicts if we attend to common neurotic anxiety in the analytic process? In its basic dimension, actual neurotic anxiety attests to failures and problems in internalization of adequate coping mechanisms for the regulation of tension. The nature of the relationship to the analyst is subject to analytic investigation that can reveal specific patterns of object relationships established in earliest childhood and repeated in the process. The nature of the internalization is open to view and its defects with regard to the progression from primary to secondary process functioning constitute symptoms evident in nonverbal repetitive behavior, in transference phenomena with the analyst, or in the subjective experience of the patient. Self constancy and object constancy and the self-soothing function are important aspects of early development, as is the mode of learning and problem solving established at the mother's knee. In the precursors of the superego, the controlling intrapsychic structures may be parental introjects, primary process presences, who must be appeased and obeyed. The structure of the ego, the precursors of the superego, and the nature of object relations may be subjected to analysis as they contribute to actual neurotic phenomena, in a developmental context that antedates conditions explained by the structural hypothesis.

What are the symptoms that must be routinely addressed in the analytic process that are not psychoneurotic symptoms? Essentially they are signals of inadequacy in tension regulation involving all the factors that move the child developmentally from primary to secondary process functioning, from the dominance of the pleasure principle to that of the reality principle. They are evident in object relations, in the tolerance and mastery of frustrations, anxiety, anger, and depression, in the mode of perception of external and internal reality, in character formation and the means of adaptive mastery. Such factors are, of course, evident to any clinical observer in the solution of oedipal conflicts but they are not all influenced by the configuration of the Oedipus complex.

Dorpat (1976) emphasizes the fact that, in the interpretation of "psychoneurotic symptoms," the tendency to explain everything on the basis of the structural hypothesis may lead to serious error. He notes that "hysterical" fear of heights may have its determinants in the grandiose belief that one can fly—may not, that is, be exclusively determined by sexual conflicts. Symptoms may be engendered by conflicts in separation-individuation, in which separation from mother carries with it mother's displeasure and pain and reverberates in the psyche of the patient. Dorpat describes a case of this type in which there were deficiencies in superego formation. With regard to separation, the mother was experienced as an introject; her displeasure, rather than the structures of an internalized code, prompted feelings of guilt. It seems appropriate to question whether, in such an instance, the patient is experiencing feelings of guilt or a fear of loss of the object or loss of the love of the object as the significant motive in his "prestructural" conflict. Such a qualification would not detract from Dorpat's main thesis, however. He further cites the contributions of Bibring (1953)—that depression may be the consequence of narcissistic frustration—and of Engel (1962)—that depression may involve ego surrender, an inability to cope. Narcissistic features require attention to the cohesiveness of the self and its disruption in response to empathic failures as well as problems of overidealization resulting from structural deficits of early childhood, as elaborated by Kohut (1971). Kernberg (1974) provides another model for addressing narcissistic aspects of personality functioning, emphasizing a primary view of narcissistic rage in contrast to its conceptualization as reactive to a failure in empathy. Derivatives of such early developmental problems may well be part of the matrix of psychoneurotic symptoms.

In the cases cited in Chapter 6, complex characterological problems were noted as significantly arising from separation-individuation experiences. Developmental patterns shaped by the exigencies of dyadic experience put their imprint on modes of relating, defense, learning, and problem solving in the service of tension regulation. In Cases 1 and 2, problems the patients encountered in child rearing prompted their return for second analyses, illuminating developmental faults and unfinished analytic business. The screaming, demanding behavior in Case 1 and the brusque, disdainful self-sufficiency in Case 2 proved to have early developmental determinants of the utmost importance. In Cases 5 and 7, a particular use of fantasy by mother and child served as an organizing factor in patterning the tension-regulatory solution to actual neurotic anxiety. In Case 6, counterphobic premature mastery was the solution to exaggerated expectations as an alternative to somatic complaints in the search for protective nurture. The fact that these modes of relating, defense, learning, and problem solving participate in the encounter with oedipal conflicts and the formation of psychoneurotic symptoms in no way reduces the importance of analyzing their dyadic roots.

Chapter 10

The Defense Transference in a Developmental Context

The defense transference, as the characterological defensive organization evident at the onset of an analysis, serves as a shield against the transference neurosis and as an important coping mechanism of the ego in the face of conflict. It is a manifestation of a central mode of behavior of the patient in relating to objects. In serving the need for adaptation, it is ego syntonic and alloplastic, persistent and repetitive. It is a pattern of response that anchors the defensive resources of the individual in his encounters with reality. Its origins are in the earliest developmental vicissitudes of life. We would describe it as an outcome of separation-individuation, as a solution to conflicts in object relations, confirmed in the crisis of the rapprochement subphase and subsequently employed in the management of oedipal conflicts and later developmental phases. In a dyadic frame of reference, this pattern of response establishes a means of tension regulation and self-soothing, and thereby sets the conditions for the solution of later intrapsychic conflicts as well. The pattern may be modified in passage through later states of

193

conflict, becoming associated with new contents. It may readily be discerned in the presenting-façade of the patient and the initial engagement with the analyst, and may become smoothly imbricated in the analytic alliance. To the extent that it facilitates adaptation, it may gain for the patient the analyst's ready approval.

In a variety of presentations around the country, we have become aware that the term is somewhat idiosyncratic to the Chicago scene, stemming as it does from Gitelson's contributions. In drawing attention to early developmental aspects of experience as they enter into the analytic process, aspects that may readily be obscured or dismissed, it is, in our experience, a helpful concept that deserves more common usage.

The phenomenon, as described up to this point, might be regarded as an unobjectionable expression of behavior found useful in the early life of the child. In fact, in this sense it fits the definition of character which Gitelson suggested: "An adaptive synthesis of forces stemming from the biological givens, the quality of the infantile environment, the psychic structures, the character of the identifications, and the mores of the social group in which later maturation and development occurs" (1963, p. 4). Why then is it designated as defense transference, with the implication that it requires analytic intervention? Because, in our view, the internalization and automatic operation of this pattern of behavior suggest that the personality itself has suffered some deformation early in its development, setting the stage for neurotic symptom formation. Through identification and compliance, the conditions for perceiving and processing experiences have become internalized, creating limits on individuation that reverberate throughout the life cycle. Attention to the *defense* transference and its roots in *separation-individuation* permits systematic access to and influence

over pathological aspects of the analytic alliance and neu-
rosogenic features in the psychic economy of the patient.
We would emphasize that we are not defining all of character development, but a specific pattern of response between child and parents that is a keynote of tension
regulation in the solution of *object relations conflicts* and
defects in the self.

We shall explore some relevant papers in the literature in an attempt to clarify our definition of the defense
transference. In 1915, Freud described in some detail a
problem frequently encountered in analysis: transference
love. Characteristically, Freud confronted the trouble-
some fact that all love was repetitive in its patterns and
that departures from the normal ways of life constituted
precisely what was essential about being in love. Nevertheless, he wrote: "There can be no doubt that the out-
break of a passionate demand for love is largely the work
of resistance. . . . She [the patient] has become quite
without insight and seems to be swallowed up in her love.
Moreover, this change quite regularly occurs precisely at
a point of time when one is having to try to bring her to
admit or remember some particularly distressing and
heavily repressed piece of her life-history" (p. 162). In
emphasizing the quality of resistance in transference
love, Freud marshalled the evidence that it was provoked
by the analytic situation and that it was lacking to a high
degree in regard for reality or consequences. He noted
that if the analyst were to succumb to the sexual demands, the patient would have only succeeded in repeating in real life what she ought to have remembered
as the psychical material for analysis. He cited as a special case the woman of elemental passion who "tolerate[d]
no surrogates" and was "accessible only to 'the logic of
soup, with dumplings for arguments'" (pp. 166-167). In
such a case, he cautioned, the analyst must resign himself

to failure, withdraw, and reflect on how a capacity for neurosis was found with such an intractable need for love. That summons for reflection is pursued here.

The insistence on gratification of the demand for love and the disregard for the conditions of the analytic situation characterize to some degree the entire group of patients Freud was describing. His attention was directed at the time to defensive maneuvers that would maintain oedipal impulses and their associated memories in an unconscious state. In the area of intrapsychic conflicts, the behavior he observed might be associated with a variety of forms of psychopathology, depending on the specifics of the case. For example, it might involve the acting out of some of the content of a transference neurosis as a defense against recognizing the oedipal conflict, or it might be a sexualized reaction defending against the acknowledgment of conflicts about homosexuality or pregenital conflicts. In any case, the abrupt, intense, and consistent demand for love reflects a blurring of the distinction between fantasy and reality, an intolerance for frustration, anxiety, and depression, and an expectation of immediate gratification. Such transference love constitutes a crisis in the analytic alliance. In its extreme form, the "intractable need for love" and "the logic of soup and dumplings" are signposts of addictive behavior, and may involve serious deficiencies of structure that would make intrapsychic oedipal conflicts themselves relatively insubstantial. In more neurotic cases, the behavior would reflect a pattern established in separation-individuation, and would constitute a defense transference in confronting oedipal conflicts.

In a recent paper on erotized transference, Blum (1973) distinguishes between erotic transference as it becomes evident in any analytic process and erotized transference as a conscious, insistent erotic transference demand. His survey of the literature indicates that an erotized transference may be a form of behavior in patients varying diagnostically from borderline and psychotic to neurotic psychopathology (he cites, in this respect, Rappaport [1956] and Swartz [1967]). It may be associated with such diverse phenomena as turbulent demands for physical contact, omnipotent strivings, dependent clinging with fear of object loss, etc. As for the genesis of an erotized transference, Blum emphasizes early developmental defects based on instinctual overstimulation and a lack of parental phase-appropriate protection and support. Narcissistic pathology is also noted, with fragility in self-esteem and self-cohesion accompanying parental insensitivity and lack of empathy. Patients with pronounced narcissistic features may have a view of their right to gratification reminiscent of Freud's (1916) description of the character of the "exceptions," for whom early deprivation and deformity serves as a justification for inordinate demands and expectations of gratification. Consistent with the theme of overstimulation in their earliest experience, there is an incidence of sexual seduction in childhood, intense masturbatory conflicts, and a family tolerance of incestuous behavior in bedroom and bathroom. Blum emphasizes that such a developmental background sanctions an erotized transference since the child has not internalized the interdictions and inhibitions of ordinary life. The erotization may serve as a resistance and defend against a variety of conflicts. In those instances where sufficient structure has formed to permit the development of a transference neurosis, the erotized transference reaction would constitute a defense transference in the sense in which we define the term. Blum quotes Freud on the danger of gratification in the analytic situation and the need to analyze the transference neurosis to enable the patient to gain mastery over his impulses. We would emphasize as well the need for analysis of the defense transference as it distorts the analytic alliance. Such a venture would engage the defense transference as an organizing principle in the patient's experience of separation-individuation and as an adaptive defense against conflicts, and help to explain how an intractable need for love has come to be joined with the capacity for neurosis.

In 1944, Gitelson reported on a pattern of chronic deviousness in the personal relations of people suffering from certain intellectualized types of narcissistic character neurosis. They remained on the periphery of real human relations, avoiding any commitment to friendship or confrontation with emotional reality. The specific incapacity in relating to objects was reflected in the analytic process in a defense transference. He described two cases to demonstrate the relationship between the defense transference and the libidinal transference, and noted that the defense transference had its origins in the early mother-child interaction.

In the first case, he received external verification of his patient's account of his mother's behavior. She was a self-deluding character who played the great lady with a display of refinement and delicacy, yet was also given to violent outbursts of rage. When her son let fly a fork at his one-and-a-half-year-old younger sister, she perceived it as his hand slipping. She bragged of never having been seen nude by her husband, but did not recognize the incongruity of relating this to her young son. When the patient was still at an early age, she would engage him in devious and solemn discussions in which erotic indulgence was a hidden agenda. Intellectuality was a form of contact and protection against the anxiety generated by the threat of recognizing secret gratification or the frustration of real longings and attendant rage. At the age of nine, the charade enacted between the two of them was epitomized by a trip they took together in which they shared a hotel room and entered into a prolonged intellectual discussion about sexual matters. In this memory from latency, the association between oedipal libidinal strivings and defense transference is apparent. Gitelson did not specifically allude to the structuring of the defense transference in the preoedipal phase, but such a view was implicit in his technical approach to both of the cases, a technical approach that involved confrontation with object relations conflict, as we shall describe below. It is important to note that Gitelson was describing a pioneering approach to defense transference that antedated the elaboration of concepts about the analytic alliance and separation-individuation. Our present assumption would be that the pattern of intellectualization as a defense transference had its origins in much earlier identification and compliance with the mother than that described by Gitelson. We would view it as originating in the patterns of communication between mother and son, the deviousness and self-delusion that Gitelson described.

In the second case, Gitelson described in a male patient an associative style of defensive hostile competitiveness expressed in proud erudition. The intellectual performance was intended to capture the interest of the analyst in a clandestine satisfaction of passive yearnings, to indulge libidinal needs without exposure to the anxiety of an emotional tie. The patient guarded against experiencing the transference neurosis, repressing the intensity of his anxiety in a fear of insanity. In an extra-analytic context, he formed a platonic relationship with a motherly woman who cared for him as a "charming son." Earlier developmental origins of the defense transference of intellectual charm and erudition were not elaborated.

Gitelson recognized the need for a technical approach to the defense transference if the analysis were not to be lost in a sea of intellectualization. A developmental context was implicit in his comment that it was not simply a matter of reductive analysis but concomitant re-education; management of the defense transference had to provide active aid to the patient in the testing of his interpersonal relations with the analyst, and the possibility of a genuine, although reality-limited, object relationship. In recognition of the alloplastic nature of the defense transference, Gitelson cautioned against the tendency to become involved in the challenge and seduction of intellectuality. He set forth as a technical necessity that the psychoanalytic situation afford the patient an opportunity for sampling a real libidinal object relationship by a judicious dosing of emotional gratification so that the delusional object could be surrendered.

Gitelson advocated and used an active technique to expose the defense transference and bring about conditions suitable for the analysis of the transference neurosis. In the first case, at the height of the patient's complaints about an absence of response to his intellectual dissertation, he responded with "Boo." He explained his intervention as a thwarting of the demand for gratification in words and ideas and regarded his "joking" response as an acknowledgment of the patient's libidinal longings and an inducement to the patient's ego to cooperate in the work of the analysis. Such a stated motive clearly related the active technique and the defense transference to our current concept of the analytic alliance. In the second case, an even more active technique was employed. At a point in the analysis when the patient complained that he had no genuine idea of the unreal analyst who sat behind him, Gitelson stood before him at the end of the hour and suggested he take a good look. His intent was to debunk the omnipotent hostile defense fantasy and "to force an awareness of the emotional reality" (Gitelson, 1944, p. 80). He felt vindicated when the patient brought in the first dream of the analysis the next day.

In his innovative approach, Gitelson recognized the nature of the defense transference: its early developmental origin in object relations that antedate the infantile neurosis, and its imbrication in the analytic alliance and in narcissistic character pathology. His active technique was, however, a psychotherapeutic and manipulative approach to the problems he delineated, as though they could be resolved by confrontation and exhortation. Such a technique was fraught with humiliation for the patient. Subsequent contributions to our knowledge of narcissism and separation-individuation have made feasible an analytic exploration of the behavior in transference phenomena and its reconstruction in a historical setting. The re-educative effect that Gitelson recognized as necessary may be accomplished by transmuting internalizations and changes in dyadic reality processing, self and object constancy, and the recognition and tolerance of affective experience.

Kris (1956), although not specifically addressing either the defense transference or the analytic alliance, described the functioning of certain types of what we would call defense transference as resistances to the establishment of the alliance. In comparing the good analytic hour to the deceptively good hour, Kris used two examples. In the first, the character defense of compliance created the illusion of a good hour as the patient attempted to gain the praise or love of the analyst, or establish a merger with him. What appeared to be insight was the mere repetition of a lesson learned from the analyst. In the second case, Kris described an intellectualizing (psychologizing) defense transference in which the analysand engaged in a pseudo self-analysis which the author attributed to hostile competitive striving in an oedipal context. Kris discussed the case examples as technical problems connected with the miscarriage and misuse of analytic insight, emphasizing that there may be an insidious defensive aspect to what appears as insight. He elucidated the implications of his observations in a manner entirely in keeping with our central thesis, namely, that the acquisition of true insight may be fostered by means of the analysis of infantile prototypes of the analytic experience. Such an analytic effort would work toward the development of secondary autonomy in the acquisition and the use of insight, as an enduring independent self analytic function. He emphasized three factors as significant in the integration of insight: (1) an ability to regress in the service of the ego; (2) the capacity for self-observation in regard to self-representations and functions; and (3) a capacity for control over the discharge of affects. His theoretical discussion cited the whole range of character development and intersystemic factors as active in the problem. We believe it can be further illuminated by a sharper focus on the phenomena of separation-individuation in the particular case under study.

Greenson (1967) emphasized the importance of attention to the analytic alliance, and implicitly engaged the issue of defense transference. He described a patient who had had an extensive experience with analysis in another city, but whose only apparent change in personality had been the acquisition of a repertoire of formulae about himself that he had learned from his analyst. His functional capacity was that of an "as if" character; the analysis had made no real impact on him. He could not tolerate the investigation of his "as if" behavior in an analytic context, and required a psychotherapeutic approach. The early developmental disorder had found its resolution in a pseudo-individuation that was adaptive and that guarded against a descent into the maelstrom.

In a second case, Greenson described a woman with whom he intensively pursued a disturbance in the analytic alliance when she came for re-analysis. The first analysis was full of unusual obscurities and featured ambivalent complaining and clinging sadomasochistic reactions to the analyst. The decision to terminate was with a mutual awareness of unfinished business. On re-analysis, Greenson noted again the patient's peculiar speech habits during the process. Whenever she experienced an upsurge of anxiety, she lapsed into incessant talking and disconnected sentences, fragmented accounts of events, occasional obscene phrases, obsessive thoughts, etc. She was apparently oblivious to her manner of speech. In the first analysis, the behavior had been partially explained as based on an identification with her mother, who had been a great character, talking to her child as though she were a grown-up before she could understand and often attacking her quiet husband with streams of anxious and hostile speech. It had also been recognized as a kind of sleep talk, a reenactment of sleeping with her parents. On re-analysis, the speech was recognized as a blurring of the real purpose of free association, a kind of spiteful obedience. It was stimulated particularly by feelings of intense hostility toward the analyst which led to fears of his destruction and loss. She would then quickly dive down into her sleep-talking which was like saying to him "I am a little child who is partly asleep and is not responsible for what is coming out of her. Don't leave me; let me sleep on with you, it is just harmless urine that is coming out of me." Greenson noted that there were other determinants for the behavior too far afield to elaborate in his discussion.

This last case report seems particularly pertinent to our purpose. The repetitive appearance of the characteristic defensive behavior to counter anxiety defines precisely the action of the defense transference in the analytic process. Its disruptive effect on the analytic alliance was clearly articulated by Greenson. The description of the clinical data used to explain the behavior, while incomplete in our view, is sufficient to demonstrate its historical and transference significance as a pattern of response based on identification with the mother to counter the threat of object loss. The connection with separation-individuation experiences may be convincingly inferred. The outcome of the original analysis attests to the importance of analyzing the defense transference. Indeed, Greenson emphasized that the course of the second analysis was strikingly different from that of the first. Analysis of what we would designate as the defense transference, whenever it appeared, resulted in a steady improvement in the analytic alliance, and a meaningful analysis of transference neurotic material.

Throughout this monograph we have presented cases that illustrate the defense transference as a characterological mode of behavior, its function in the analytic process, and the need to analyze its early developmental origins. Our major hypothesis may now be stated quite simply. The defense transference is the individual's characteristic pattern of behavior with respect to object relations, and serves as a defense against neurotic conflict. It is itself the outcome of separation-individuation and self conflicts, and operates thereafter as an adaptive solution to those early conflicts. Internalization of the pattern as a complex coping mechanism protects the child from unmanageable tension states. The solution of the rapprochement subphase serves as an organizer of the defense transference, establishing the limits and distortions of and the necessary support systems for the developing ego functions. It is in these early phases of development that actual neurotic anxiety is encountered in its genetic forms. The pattern of behavior in relation to objects operates as a regulatory mechanism in the tolerance and control of tension states, and contributes to the capacities for self and object constancy, self-soothing, and dyadic reality processing. Psychological development in childhood may thus be conceptualized as a two-stage process—an initial phase of separation-individuation and internalization of self- and object representations, and a superstructure emerging out of the resolution and internalization of the Oedipus complex with its potential for intrapsychic conflicts. As a solution to object relations conflict, the defense transference determines the conditions for actual neurotic anxiety and influences profoundly the conditions for the development of later psychoneurotic problems. Our definition of this pattern of behavior as *defense* transference is thus contingent on its operation as a defense against neurotic conflict. We wish to underline the definition in this regard, in order to emphasize that we are not suggesting a focus of interest in unusual cases of severe character pathology, but one that is important in any analytic process. We readily acknowledge that in *severe character problems, the oedipal phase may be poorly cathected and the pattern of behavior evolving out of separation-individuation would exist and be open to analytic intervention without constituting a defense transference.* It would then be, more simply, a solution to object relations conflicts and a character defense not related to oedipal transference. It is worthy of note in this regard that actual neurotic problems associated with the consequences of particular separation-individuation experiences may coexist with psychoneurotic problems, and, in the absence of a conceptualization that includes the entire sweep of development, sterile arguments may be entered into about what is the diagnosis and appropriate treatment of these problems. On the basis of our investigations and clinical experience, we are convinced that this characterological pattern of behavior demands careful definition and analysis of its determinants in separation-individuation as much in classical psychoneurotic cases as in the range of character problems encountered in the widening scope of psychoanalysis.

Within the paradigm of development set forth by Mahler, a number of factors may be adduced as contributing to the solution of the rapprochement crisis—a solution which, in our view, constitutes the defense transference. Essentially, they bear on the effect of trauma in object relations in the earliest phases of development. The complex interactions that have their issue in the solution to the rapprochement crisis cannot be overemphasized as to their importance. The time of decisive conflict in object relations is an important genetic determinant. The earlier the conflict, the more profound its effect. Traumatic factors, such as the loss of the object, consistent overgratification or deprivation, or inconsistent responses based on a lack of empathy may have a shock effect if narrowly focused in a time slot that coincides with the development or consolidation of particular ego functions, a "critical period" genetically in the life of an individual. A persistent experience of stimuli that provide other than optimal frustration would constitute a devastating strain trauma, distorting the entire process of development. The amount of stimulation, the degree of preparation for it, and the availability of substitute parental figures to mediate stress and provide alternatives for identification all have their significance. Libidinal, aggressive, and narcissistic lines of development converge in separation-individuation in their various stages and manifestations. Their individual effects and interactions may be studied. Narcissistic features may predominate, with the development of the drives engaged as fragmentation products (Kohut, 1977). Particular drive aspects may be submerged or obliterated in response to fears of loss of the object and its internalization as a harsh primary process presence. The developmental potential of language and logic may be facilitated or perverted. Early effects of parental response on gender identity may be a significant shaping force. Furthermore, Freud's concept of the complementary series between constitutional factors and environmental contributions assumes particular relevance in these early events. The dovetailing of outer events and inner psychic organization that one must reconstruct in the analysis of early determinants of patterns of behavior demands careful investigation and critical attention to the applicability of new paradigms of development. It is necessary to guard against a new formulary approach or an imaginative exercise in which the means and explanations generated are accepted simply on the grounds of faith or therapeutic efficacy for the individual. Derivatives of early childhood behavior patterns in the analytic process tax to the utmost the analyst's capacities for introspection and empathy, and his readiness to remain open to inconsistencies and surprises, whatever their source, for the special illuminating effects that they provide.

The critical and technical issues raised above have, in one form or another, already engaged the interest of a number of investigators. The available yield of recent contributions to the literature permits some initial illustrations of a developmental view of defense transferences. Fenichel (1941), in a prescient grasp of the issues involved, suggested in his own formulation of defense transference that a special defensive attitude is forced on the individual by a particular historical situation in earliest childhood in which the specific ingredients have a decisive influence in creating an enduring pattern of behavior that is uniquely appropriate for the individual and repetitively expedient. In a particular individuation experience, the special pattern that emerges mediates as effectively as possible between the instinctual forces involved, the basic models facilitating identification or oppositional trends, and the controlling behavior of the significant caretaker.

Brodey (1965) describes an early and extreme form of such pathology in a child of narcissistic parents. The child exists as an "as if" entity. The mother responds to him only when his behavior corresponds to her image of him. His self-image is thereby generated by his mother's expectations. Spontaneous behavior is a threat. His pseudo personality reflects mother's views and is not supported by the growth and experience of the child himself. In its most extreme form, individuation of the variety described here would create an "as if" personality totally dependent for its structure and sustenance on an external object. A less formidably unempathic mother may create a lesser degree of pseudo-individuation to serve as a defense transference on the order of the phenomena described in Gitelson's examples of narcissistic characters.

Masterson and Rinsley (1975) in their view of borderline states within the framework of separation-individuation describe a central dynamic of paradoxical responses on the part of the mother. Steps in the direction of maturation and development are experienced by the mother as a threat. Regressive trends are encouraged and

rewarded (in the sense of Stone's [1961] primordial transference) and the development of autonomous functions
and self-object differentiation is problematic and seriously compromised by any separation. Splitting and fragmentation may predominate in conflicts, with their origin
at the earliest stage of differentiation from the initial
symbiosis. The development of instincts may be blocked
or impaired or segmentally hypertrophied in perverse
discharge phenomena mobilized by efforts at self-soothing. Again, the pattern here described in its extreme
form, in which the mother encourages regression, may
exist in modified variants and be mobilized by specific
stages of development or instinctual derivatives significant to the mother. In less serious disruptions of development, it would constitute a defense transference.

Modell (1975) describes what he designates a narcissistic defense against affects, which differs from isolation
in that it is directed against object relations rather than
specific component instincts. The trauma here consists
of an interaction between mother and child in which the
mother fails to accept the child's separateness and autonomy, engaging in disruptive and intrusive behavior
ostensibly in the interest of the child's growth. In a developmental process this results in a precocious but frag-
ile establishment of a sense of self with an accompanying
illusion of self-sufficiency. In the presence of such a narcissistic defense, the analytic effort is experienced as essentially intrusive and controlling.

In the sphere of narcissistic pathology, Kohut (1971)
describes two major forms of psychopathology on a developmental line. The earliest rests on unempathic mothering, a deprivation with regard to mirroring responses
that would ordinarily confirm the developing resources
of the child and contribute to the development of a cohesive self. The child raised in such a setting is fixated

on a need for self objects to perform a function which he has not adequately internalized, and is vulnerable to experiences of fragmentation when faced with unempathic reactions or separations. At a later nodal point in development, if the process of overidealization of the parents, with its gradual disillusionments and structured accretions, is suddenly and traumatically disrupted by excessive de-idealization or loss, a defect in the ego ideal may occur and be manifested in the vicissitudes of idealizing transferences in the analytic situation. In his innovative investigations, Kohut describes these phenomena as occurring in a separate line of development, that of narcissism. Narcissistic traumata may mobilize patterns of behavior described by Kohut as mirroring or idealizing transferences, which, as forms of relating to objects, express adaptive approaches to a defect in narcissistic structure. We would suggest that, as coping mechanisms, they may serve as a characterological defense with regard to libidinal and aggressive conflicts. Kohut points out that where the narcissistic pathology is primary and predominant, the drive manifestations may be fragmentation products of central narcissistic reactions, as, for example, in perverse behavior, in which the discharge of tension is paramount as a form of self-soothing, or in narcissistic rage, in which the aggression is an ineffectual expression of the child's loss of hope of fulfillment of his goals. Patterns of integration of narcissistic and libidinal development require careful observation and research. Narcissistic patterns of relating may serve as a defense transference depending on their intensity and function in specific childhood experiences.

Khan (1974) advances his own generative concept of cumulative trauma. He emphasizes that the mother serves a function as a protective shield against stimuli. Failures in this protective function during critical periods in the infant's life or as a persistent deprivation result in an accumulation of traumatic experiences. The child must prematurely assume the task of maintaining a stimulus barrier for himself, with a forced growth of certain ego functions in the service of defense and survival, while other functions are suppressed and stunted. Khan suggests that in such cases separation-individuation is disrupted by a collusive relationship with the mother characterized by excessive sensitivity to her moods and problems with the tolerance and mastery of aggression. His emphasis is thus on a specific pattern of premature mastery.

Parental expectations and techniques for exercising control over the acquisition and integration of new skills set up stressful foci in object relations which result in myriad forms of solution. In the case described in Chapter 3, the effect of parental expectations of premature mastery, as a narcissistic fulfillment for the parents, was traced in its evolution into a counterphobic approach to life. This behavior resulted in considerable adaptive success but was marred by problems in the secure integration of learning, satisfaction in work and sex, and independent functioning. In our discussion of defense transference in the context of transference love and erotized transference, the emphasis was on overstimulation and seduction as parental contributions to the structuring of reality. In the cases cited by Kris, compliance was the major focus, with deep roots in a wish for merger or the wish for praise or love as derivatives of a later stage in development. The rapprochement subphase is an organizing crossroads at which the prevailing pattern emerges. The examples offered in this chapter are merely illustrative and intended to emphasize the need for particular definition and analysis of the development of this particular mode of behavior in specific cases.

To lend dramatic emphasis to the significance of the analysis of the defense transference for the therapeutic efficacy of the analytic process, we shall now enlist the concept of the negative therapeutic reaction in what may at first seem a strange alliance. Asch (1976) discusses the negative therapeutic reaction within the frame of reference of Mahler's investigation of individuation. He quotes Freud's classical explanation in the "Ego and the Id" (1923) for failures in analysis in spite of correct interpretive work, namely, "a moral factor, a sense of guilt which is finding its satisfaction in the illness and refuses to give up the punishment of suffering" (p. 49). He further notes that Freud had already utilized such an explanation in 1916 for the so-called "criminals from a sense of guilt," those wrecked by success, and the fate neuroses: "It is the forces of conscience which forbid the subject to gain the long hoped-for advantage from the fortunate change in reality" (p. 318). Freud's explanation rested on the paradigm of oedipal conflict. Asch, on the basis of his own clinical investigations, emphasizes the earlier roots of the problem in patterns of behavior stemming from the struggle for individuation. He describes three varieties of earlier genetic determinants that, in their behavioral consequences, may be explanatory for negative therapeutic reactions and would constitute defense transferences by our definition—to the extent, that is, they are engaged as defenses against oedipal conflict. The first is an interaction with the parent requiring suffering and renunciation as the price of love. The parent idealizes a life of suffering and lack of gratification and exists as an introject in the psyche of the patient, resisting his improvement and, particularly, interpretations directed at the removal of obstacles to pleasure. In relation to the introject, the function of the treatment is penance, not cure. The behavior is zealously maintained because any change in the direction of improvement threatens a critically important archaic object relationship. In fact, Asch emphasizes that in one patient, the mother, dead for several years, was experienced as though still alive, as a primary process presence in the ego ideal. In another instance, efforts to defeat analytic interventions were undertaken by the patient in his role as the good son protecting his relationship with an ethereal mother against a skillful adversary. Splits in the transference might well engage the analyst himself in the unconscious role of the mother as well, in the reenactment of a childhood scene.

A second pattern elucidated by Asch is that of unconscious guilt as a result of dyadic conflicts. It is characterized by a conviction of personal responsibility for mother's mutilation and disease, as a consequence of separation fantasies and tales involving the patient's birth. Guilt may also be engendered by destructive fantasies about siblings still in the womb. Subsequent separations are associated with traumatic dissolution of the mother-child symbiosis. An intense narcissistic attachment exists with a special intolerance for rage. Behaviorally, there is urgency in the need for contact to maintain the fantasy of a symbiotic union and to control aggression. Poor self-object differentiation is an obvious concomitant and the exacerbation of symptoms in the terminal phase is a natural consequence. Asch notes the similarity to Modell's (1975) concept of separation guilt.

Asch's third genetic description is of a negative therapeutic reaction based on a defense against symbiotic fusion. Negativism in oral and anal modes preserves what is inside the child and protects him from his mother's self-aggrandizement and engulfment. Any analytic effort is perceived as domination. There is danger in doing anything in accordance with the analyst's understanding because it is for mother and not for himself. At a deeper level, the passive wish for fusion may constitute the threat. Insistence on free association in such a case would constitute an intolerable demand. Every aspect of the analytic contract is the focus of a struggle that repeats the past in a defense transference fraught with constant danger for any therapeutic intervention.

Asch emphasizes the decisive role of defects in separation-individuation in the negative therapeutic reaction. Technically, he advises the careful and patient analysis of every dimension of these patterns of behavior as they enter the analytic process. Introjects in the ego ideal, in the superego, and in ambivalently cathected self-representations must be modified in passage as the patient attempts to mold the analyst into his infantile prototypes. The multiply determined need to fail requires particular investigation as to its sources in early obstacles to individuation. Calm observation and understanding may provide the possibility of internalization of a real relationship that counters the effects of hostile introjects. Asch notes the special problems of countertransference with such patients and the fact that failures in tact and patience may be put to good use by identifying the pattern in which they occur.

The technical approach outlined by Asch, although it is addressed to special cases, is consonant with our own view of the suitable treatment for defense transferences. We would add the concept of transmuting internalizations to elaborate his description of the effect of the analyst's small failures in empathy when these are followed by an interpretive grasp of their occurrence and effects in the context of a reconstruction of the past. The transmuting internalization results from a simultaneous exercise of analytic understanding and structure building. Asch's emphasis on the fact that it is often not until the termination phase that the most effective work can be done on the profound and stubborn issues involved in the negative therapeutic reaction confirms our own findings on the significance of the termination phase for a careful analysis of the defense transference and the analytic alliance. The exacerbation of symptoms during this phase directs attention to the wish to preserve the relationship in the face of final separation, highlighting its infantile precursors.

In conclusion, we shall shift to a wider and happier perspective; the creative potential inherent in the exploration of the earliest stages of development as their derivatives appear in the analytic process. The explanatory power of the Oedipus complex in understanding the neuroses and intrapsychic conflicts of man has been and remains a major achievement of psychoanalytic investigation. Its significance is not diminished by later discoveries but must be integrated with them. In this monograph, we have cited the work of many analysts who have extended their explorations beyond the hard-won insights into the vicissitudes and consequences of the oedipal phase. In our view, the confrontation with the origins of structure and the effort to understand the early development of intrapsychic conditions for neurotic symptom formation and character pathology have followed an inexorable course in psychoanalytic practice. There is an inherent logic in the fact that deeper developmental layers were exposed in later investigations. Our follow-up studies have highlighted this process of discovery. We have demonstrated to our satisfaction the usefulness of such studies, as an experimental procedure, in sharpening the focus on accomplishments and failures in analytic process and outcome and, thereby, providing data for hypotheses and conclusions about the significance of early childhood derivatives in psychoanalytic theory and technique. We have emphasized the potential for integrating existing knowledge and pursued our own approach to the task. In setting forth the exciting prospects for such research, we invite the collaboration of research teams in other analytic centers in expanding the yield, testing the results, and accelerating the process of discovery and consolidation of analytic knowledge.

References

Arlow, J. (1975), The structural hypothesis—theoretical considerations. *Psychoanal. Quart.,* 44:509-525.

Asch, S. (1976), Varieties of negative therapeutic reaction and problems of technique. *J. Amer. Psychoanal. Assn.,* 24:383-408.

Basch, M. (1976), Theory formation in Chapter VII: A critique. *J. Amer. Psychoanal. Assn.,* 24:61-100.

Bibring, E. (1953), The mechanics of depression. In: *Affective Disorders,* ed. P. Greenacre. New York: International Universities Press, pp. 13-48.

Blos, P. (1967), The second individuation process in adolescence. *The Psychoanalytic Study of the Child,* 22:162-186. New York: International Universities Press.

Blum, H. (1973), The concept of erotized transference. *J. Amer. Psychoanal. Assn.,* 21:61-76.

Brodey, W. (1965), On the dynamics of narcissism: 1. Externalization and early ego development. *The Psychoanalytic Study of the Child,* 20:165-193. New York: International Universities Press.

Deutsch, H. (1959), Psychoanalytic therapy in the light of follow-up. *J. Amer. Psychoanal. Assn.,* 7:445-458.

Dewald, P. (1976), Transference regression and real experience in the psychoanalytic process. *Psychoanal. Quart.,* 45:213-230.

Dorpat, T. (1976), Structural conflict and object relations conflict. *J. Amer. Psychoanal. Assn.,* 24:855-874.

Engel, G. (1962), Anxiety and depression-withdrawal: The primary affects of unpleasure. *Internat J. Psycho-Anal.,* 43:89-97.

Fenichel, O. (1941), Problems of psychoanalytic technique. *Psychoanal. Quart.,* 10:66-69.

Firestein, S. K. (1978), *Termination in Psychoanalysis.* New York: International Universities Press.

217

Fleming, J. (1972), Early object deprivation and transference phenomena: The working alliance. *Psychoanal. Quart.*, 41:23-49.

French, T. (1954), *The Integration of Behavior. Vol. 2: The Integrative Process in Dreams.* Chicago: University of Chicago Press.

—— (1958), *The Reintegrative Process in a Psychoanalytic Treatment.* Chicago: University of Chicago Press.

Freud, S. (1912), Types of onset of neurosis. *Standard Edition,* 12:231-238. London: Hogarth Press, 1958.

—— (1914), Remembering, repeating and working through. *Standard Edition,* 12:147-156. London: Hogarth Press, 1958.

—— (1915), Observations on transference love. *Standard Edition,* 12:159-171. London: Hogarth Press, 1958.

—— (1916), Some character types met with in psychoanalytic work: The exceptions. *Standard Edition,* 14:311-333. London: Hogarth Press, 1957.

—— (1916-1917), Introductory Lectures on Psycho-Analysis. *Standard Edition,* 15 & 16. London: Hogarth Press, 1963.

—— (1923), The ego and the id. *Standard Edition* 19:5-63. London: Hogarth Press, 1961.

—— (1926), Inhibitions, Symptoms and Anxiety. *Standard Edition,* 20:87-175. London: Hogarth Press, 1959.

—— (1933), New Introductory Lectures on Psycho-Analysis. *Standard Edition,* 22:5-182. London: Hogarth Press, 1964.

—— (1937), Analysis terminable and interminable. *Standard Edition,* 23:216-253. London: Hogarth Press, 1964.

Gedo, J., & Goldberg, A. (1973), *Models of the Mind: A Psychoanalytic Theory.* Chicago: University of Chicago Press.

Gitelson, M. (1944), Intellectuality in the defense transference. In: *Psychoanalysis: Science and Profession.* New York: International Universities Press, pp. 62-98.

—— (1962), The first phase of psychoanalysis. In: Symposium: The Curative Factors in Psychoanalysis. *Internat. J. Psycho-Anal.,* 43:194-234.

—— (1963), On the problem of character neurosis. *J. Hillside Hosp.,* 12:3-17.

Greenacre, P. (1971), *Emotional Growth,* Vol. 1. New York: International Universities Press.

Greenson, R. (1967), *The Technique and Practice of Psychoanalysis.* New York: International Universities Press.

Hendrick, I. (1942), Instinct and the ego during infancy. *Psychoanal. Quart.,* 11:33-47.

Holt, R. (1975), The past and future of ego psychology. *Psychoanal. Quart.,* 44:550-576.

Hurn, H., Reporter (1973), Panel "On the Fate of the Transference

After the Termination of Analysis." *J. Amer. Psychoanal. Assn.*, 21:182-192.

Kernberg, O. (1974), Contrasting viewpoints regarding the nature and psychoanalytic treatment of narcissistic personalities: A preliminary communication. *J. Amer. Psychoanal. Assn.*, 22:255-267.

Khan, M. (1974), *The Privacy of the Self*. London: Hogarth Press.

Kohut, H. (1966), Forms and transformations of narcissism. *J. Amer. Psychoanal. Assn.*, 14:243-272.

—— (1971), *The Analysis of the Self*. New York: International Universities Press.

—— (1977), *The Restoration of the Self*. New York: International Universities Press.

Kramer, M. (1959), On the continuation of the analytic process after psychoanalysis (a self observation). *Internat. J. Psycho-Anal.*, 40:17-25.

Kris, E. (1956), Some vicissitudes of insight in psychoanalysis. *Internat. J. Psycho-Anal.*, 37:445-455.

Kubie, L. (1941), The repetitive core of neurosis. *Psychoanal. Quart.*, 10:23-43.

Leites, N. (1971), *The New Ego*. New York: Science House.

Loewald, H. (1962), Internalization, separation, mourning and the superego. *Psychoanal. Quart.*, 31:483-504.

Mahler, M. (1972a), On the first three subphases of the separation-individuation process. *Internat. J. Psycho-Anal.*, 53:333-338.

—— (1972b), Rapprochement subphase of the separation-individuation process. *Psychoanal. Quart.*, 41:487-506.

—— Pine, F., and Bergman, A. (1975), *The Psychological Birth of the Human Infant*. New York: Basic Books.

Masterson, J., & Rinsley, D. (1975), The borderline syndrome: The role of the mother in the genesis and psychic structure of the borderline personality. *Internat. J. Psycho-Anal.*, 56:163-178.

Miller, A., Isaacs, K., & Haggard, E. (1965), On the nature of the observing function of the ego. *Brit. J. Med. Psychol.*, 38:161-169.

Modell, A. (1975), A narcissistic defense against affects and the illusion of self-sufficiency. *Internat. J. Psycho-Anal.*, 56:275-282.

—— (1976), "The holding environment" and the therapeutic action of psychoanalysis. *J. Amer. Psychoanal. Assn.*, 24:285-308.

Norman, H., Blacker, K., Oremland, J., & Barrett, W. (1976), The fate of the transference neurosis after termination of a satisfactory analysis. *J. Amer. Psychoanal. Assn.*, 24:471-498.

Oremland, J., Blacker, K., & Norman, H. (1975), Incompleteness in "successful" psychoanalysis: A follow-up study. *J. Amer. Psychoanal. Assn.*, 23:819-844.

Peterfreund, E. (1975), The need for a new general theoretical frame of reference for psychoanalysis. *Psychoanal. Quart.*, 44:534-549.

Pfeffer, A. (1959), A procedure for evaluating the results of psychoanalysis. *J. Amer. Psychoanal. Assn.*, 7:418-444.

—— Reporter (1961a), Panel on "Research in Psychoanalysis." *J. Amer. Psychoanal. Assn.*, 9:562-571.

—— (1961b), Follow-up study of a satisfactory analysis. *J. Amer. Psychoanal. Assn.*, 9:698-718.

—— (1963), The meaning of the analyst after analysis—a contribution to the theory of therapeutic results. *J. Amer. Psychoanal. Assn.*, 11:229-244.

Rangell, L. (1970), Discussion of "The Intrapsychic Process and its Analysis: A Recent Line of Thought and its Current Implications." Plenary Session. *Internat. J. Psycho-Anal.*, 51:195-210.

Rappaport, E. (1956), The management of an erotized transference. *Psychoanal. Quart.*, 25:515-529.

Robbins, F., & Sadow, L. (1974), A developmental hypothesis of reality processing. *J. Amer. Psychoanal. Assn.*, 22:344-363.

Sadow, L., Gedo, J. E., Miller, J. A., Pollock, G. H., Sabshin, M., & Schlessinger, N. (1968), The process of hypothesis change in three early psychoanalytic concepts. *J. Amer. Psychoanal. Assn.*, 16:245-273.

Schafer, R. (1968), *Aspects of Internalization*. New York: International Universities Press.

—— (1976), *A New Language for Psychoanalysis*. New Haven: Yale University Press.

Seitz, P. (1968), Cycles and subcycles in the analytic process. Presented to the Chicago Psychoanalytic Society, May, 28.

Stone, L. (1961), The psychoanalytic situation. New York: International Universities Press.

Swartz, J. (1967), The erotized transference and other transference problems. *Psychoanal. Forum*, 3:319-321.

Waelder, R. (1956), Freud and the history of science. *J. Amer. Psychoanal. Assn.*, 4:602-613.

Wallerstein, R., & Sampson, H. (1971), Issues in research in the psychoanalytic process. *Internat. J. Psycho-Anal.*, 52:11-51.

Winestein, M., Reporter (1973), Panel on "The Experience of Separation-Individuation in Infancy and Its Reverberations through the Course of Life. 1: Infancy and Childhood." *J. Amer. Psychoanal. Assn.*, 21:135-154.

Zetzel, E. (1964), The use and misuse of psychoanalysis in psychiatric evaluation and psychotherapeutic practice. In: *The Proceedings of the 6th International Congress of Psychotherapy*, Part 1. London: S. Karger, pp. 101-109.

—— (1965a), The theory of therapy in relation to a developmental model of the psychic apparatus. *Internat. J. Psycho-Anal.*, 46:39-52.

——— (1965b), Depression and the incapacity to bear it. In: *Drives, Affects, Behavior,* Vol. 2, ed. M. Schur. New York: International Universities Press, pp. 243-274.

INDEX